*Empowering Women through Wellness*
*and Self-Care*

**HANNA OLIVAS**

*Along With 26 Inspiring Authors*

ISBN: 978-1-966798-42-2

# TABLE OF CONTENTS

# INTRODUCTION

Welcome to *SHE GLOWS: Empowering Women through Wellness and Self-Care*. You hold in your hands a powerful invitation—an invitation to reconnect with yourself, to nurture your mind, body, and spirit, and to embrace a life filled with vibrant wellness and radiant energy.

In today's fast-paced world, it's easy to put yourself last. The demands of daily life—balancing careers, relationships, and responsibilities—can leave little room for self-care. But what if taking time for yourself wasn't a luxury, but a necessity? What if investing in your well-being could transform every area of your life?

That's where *SHE GLOWS* comes in. This book is a celebration of women who have discovered the transformative power of wellness and self-care. Through inspiring personal stories and expert insights, this collection offers practical strategies and heartfelt wisdom that can help you prioritize yourself and embrace the radiant glow that resides within you.

Each chapter of *SHE GLOWS* is a journey—an exploration of what it means to nurture your body, mind, and spirit, and to cultivate a life full of vitality and joy. You'll read about women from diverse backgrounds, each of whom has overcome unique challenges on their path to wellness. From their stories, you'll discover that there is no one-size-fits-all approach to self-care. It's about finding what works for *you*.

This book isn't just about physical health; it's about holistic well-being. It's about finding balance, setting boundaries, and embracing practices that nourish you at every level—emotionally, mentally, and spiritually. Inside, you'll find practical tips for integrating wellness into your daily routine, expert advice from nutritionists, fitness trainers, and mental health professionals, as well as powerful empowerment tools to help you grow and thrive.

*SHE GLOWS* is more than a book. It's a community. A community of women who have learned the importance of self-care, and who are here to share their wisdom with you. Whether you're just beginning your wellness journey or looking to deepen your practices, this guide will offer you the support, encouragement, and inspiration you need to thrive.

It's time to reclaim your health, embrace your glow, and live a life that honors the amazing woman you are. Let this book be your companion as you embark on a journey of self-discovery, empowerment, and radiant well-being.

You deserve it. You are worthy of this glow.

## Hanna Olivas

Founder and CEO of SHE RISES STUDIOS

https://www.linkedin.com/company/she-rises-studios/
https://www.facebook.com/sherisesstudios
https://www.instagram.com/sherisesstudios_llc/
www.SheRisesStudios.com

Author, Speaker, and Founder. Hanna was born and raised in Las Vegas, Nevada, and has paved her way to becoming one of the most influential women of 2022. Hanna is the co-founder of She Rises Studios and the founder of the Brave & Beautiful Blood Cancer Foundation. Her journey started in 2017 when she was first diagnosed with Multiple Myeloma, an incurable blood cancer. Now more than ever, her focus is to empower other women to become leaders because The Future is Female. She is currently traveling and speaking publicly to women to educate them on entrepreneurship, leadership, and owning the female power within.

# A Journey of Radiance, Transformation, and Love

### By Hanna Olivas

There's a kind of light that comes from within, a glow that doesn't fade, even when life gets hard. It's a light that comes from deep inside your soul, ignited by every experience—every laugh, every tear, every heartbreak, every victory. That's the glow I'm talking about. The glow that comes from being a woman who has walked through fire and emerged not burned, but brighter than ever. That's what it means to glow.

When I think about glowing, I don't just think about happiness or joy, though those are certainly part of it. To me, glowing is deeper than that. It's about resilience. It's about rising even when life tries to knock you down. It's about loving yourself through all the ups and downs, and trusting that no matter what happens, you will shine. "You don't need perfect circumstances to glow; you just need to believe in your light."

My glow didn't come from a life that was easy. It came from the challenges I've faced, the tears I've cried, and the moments when I felt like giving up. I've had moments where I questioned everything—my purpose, my path, my strength. But each time, I was reminded that the glow inside me never dimmed. It was always there, waiting for me to believe in it again.

I remember a time when I felt like the light inside me was flickering, barely there. Life was heavy. I was trying to juggle everything—business, family, health—and I felt like I was failing at all of it. The world felt dark, and I wasn't sure if I could keep going. But then, in a moment of quiet, I realized something. "The glow isn't something you have to earn—it's something you are." That was a game-changer for me. I didn't have to be perfect, or strong, or have it all together to glow. I just had to show up as I was, in all my messiness and imperfection, and let my light shine.

There's something so beautiful about a woman who knows her worth, even when the world tries to tell her she's not enough. That's the essence of glowing. It's about owning your story, every part of it, and recognizing that it's all part of what makes you shine. The struggles don't dim your light—they enhance it. They add depth, richness, and character to your glow. "Your scars don't make you less—they make you luminous."

I think back to the women who have inspired me the most in life—my mom and my grandmother. They aren't Latina, but they taught me what it means to embrace my heritage, to love myself deeply, and to stand tall in my truth. They had their own struggles, but they never let those struggles take away their light. They showed me that even in the darkest moments, you can choose to glow. They taught me that "your light is something no one can take away from you, not even life's hardest battles."

There have been so many moments in my life where I've had to choose to glow, even when it felt impossible. I've had to dig deep, to find that inner fire when everything around me felt cold. And let me tell you, there have been tears—so many tears. I've cried out of frustration, out of heartbreak, and out of pure exhaustion. But here's the thing: "Tears don't dim your glow; they water your soul, making your light even brighter."

I used to think that glowing meant always being positive, always having it together, always smiling. But I've learned that glowing is so much more than that. It's about being real. It's about showing up, even when you feel like you're falling apart. It's about owning your story, the good, the bad, and everything in between. "Authenticity is what makes you glow—it's what makes your light undeniable."

There's laughter in this journey too, though. Oh, the laughter! Sometimes, the best medicine is to laugh in the face of the chaos, to find joy in the small things, even when everything feels overwhelming. I've had moments where I've laughed until I cried, not because everything was perfect, but because in that moment, I chose joy. "Laughter is the spark that keeps your glow alive, even when life tries to put it out."

I've found that glowing is about letting go, too. Letting go of the need to control everything, letting go of the expectations that weigh you down, and letting go of the fear that you're not enough. "When you release what no longer serves you, you make room for your light to shine even brighter." It's been a journey for me to learn that. I've had to unlearn the idea that my worth is tied to how much I can do, how successful I am, or how well I can juggle all the roles I play. My worth, and my glow, comes from simply being me.

One of the biggest lessons I've learned about glowing is that it's not about perfection. It's about progress. There have been so many times when I've felt like I wasn't enough—like I wasn't doing enough, being enough, or succeeding enough. But here's the truth: "You don't have to be perfect to glow; you just have to be willing to grow." Every step forward, no matter how small, adds to your glow. Every time you choose to keep going, even when it's hard, your light shines a little brighter.

I've also learned that glowing is contagious. When you let your light shine, you give others permission to do the same. There's something magical about seeing another woman step into her light, owning her power, and radiating from within. It's like a ripple effect—your glow inspires others to find their own light, to step into their own power, and to shine in ways they never thought possible. "When you glow, you light up the world around you."

One of my favorite mantras is "Glow through what you go through." It's a reminder that even when life gets tough, even when you're in the midst of a storm, you can still shine. Your glow isn't dependent on your circumstances—it's something that comes from within. It's a part of who you are. And when you tap into that inner light, nothing can dim it.

There's a beauty in glowing that comes from embracing all of who you are. The parts of yourself you love, and the parts you're still working on. The moments when you feel strong, and the moments when you feel vulnerable. The successes, and the failures. It's all part of your glow.

"Your glow comes from loving yourself exactly as you are, in this moment, without needing to change a thing."

But glowing isn't just about yourself. It's about how you show up in the world, how you love others, how you share your light with those around you. "When you glow, you become a beacon for others who are searching for their own light." I've seen this in my own life. The more I embrace my glow, the more I'm able to inspire and uplift the people around me. And that, to me, is the most beautiful part of glowing.

I used to think that glowing was about achieving a certain level of success or reaching a particular goal. But now, I see that glowing is a way of being. It's how you choose to live your life, how you choose to show up for yourself and for others, and how you choose to love—deeply, fully, and unconditionally. "Glowing is about choosing love in every moment, especially when it's hard."

Love is at the heart of glowing. Self-love, love for others, and love for life itself. When you live from a place of love, your glow is undeniable. You radiate from the inside out, and that light touches everything and everyone around you. "Love is what fuels your glow, and when you lead with love, your light becomes unstoppable."

And so, as I reflect on what it means to glow, I realize that it's not just about the light that shines on the outside—it's about the fire that burns within. It's about the strength, the resilience, the love, and the joy that lives in your soul. It's about choosing to rise, even when life tries to bring you down. It's about laughing through the tears, loving through the pain, and shining through the darkness.

"She glows not because her life is perfect, but because she has chosen to rise, to love, to laugh, and to shine—no matter what." That's the truth of it. That's the essence of glowing.

So, here's to every woman who has felt like her light was dimming. Here's to every woman who has questioned whether she is enough.

Here's to every woman who has walked through the fire and come out the other side, stronger and brighter than ever before. You are enough. You are radiant. You are powerful. And your glow is something the world needs.

"Glow, not because life is easy, but because you are unbreakable." That's the mantra I live by now. It's a reminder that no matter what happens, my light will never go out. It's a reminder that I am powerful beyond measure, that I am loved, and that I am worthy of everything my heart desires.

Because that's who I am. I am a woman who glows, and I will never let my light be dimmed by fear, by doubt, or by the challenges life throws my way. "She glows because she has learned to embrace her imperfections, her struggles, and her victories with grace and courage."

So here's to you, to every woman reading this. I want you to know that your glow is your superpower. It's what makes you unique, what makes you strong, and what makes you beautiful. Don't ever let anyone tell you that your light is too bright or that you need to dim it to make others comfortable. "Your light is meant to shine, to inspire, to heal, and to uplift the world around you."

Let your glow be a reminder of your strength, your resilience, and your capacity to love. Let it be a beacon for others who are searching for their own light. And most of all, let it be a celebration of who you are—a woman who radiates from within, who shines brightly in the face of adversity, and who glows with love, laughter, and purpose.

You are radiant. You are powerful. You are unstoppable. And as long as you believe in your glow, there's nothing you can't achieve.

"She glows, not because life is without storms, but because she has become the light within them."

And that, my beautiful sister, is why you will always glow.

## Paula C Lamb

Health & Personal Development Coach, Podcaster

https://www.linkedin.com/in/paulalamb/
https://www.facebook.com/BeyondtoFreedom/
https://www.instagram.com/beyondtofreedom
https://linktr.ee/podcasterpaula
https://www.youtube.com/@knowingmeknowingyouwithpaula

Meet Paula Lamb, a South African expat now calling Vancouver, Canada, home. With a background in the service industry, physical fitness, nutrition, and personal growth coaching, she now focuses on guiding individuals toward holistic well-being—spiritual, mental, and physical—through life coaching and her podcast, Beyond to Freedom. Paula's mission is to empower and inspire her listeners and clients to move beyond whatever is holding them back and take actionable steps toward embracing freedom. In her first co-authored anthology, She Stands Strong: 30 Personal Stories of Strength & Resilience, Paula shares a deeply personal chapter on the importance of making friends with fear and doubt. In this next co-authored chapter in She Glows she hopes to inspire readers to take small, meaningful actions to nurture their spiritual, mental and physical well-being, ultimately finding lasting peace and joy. Her message is clear: glowing from the inside out isn't just possible—it's your birthright.

# Beyond Skin Deep:
# The Power of Mindful Radiance

By Paula C Lamb

Have you ever wondered what it truly means to 'glow from the inside out'? Or when you hear phrases like 'Your health is your wealth' or 'Fit for life,' what comes to mind? For me, the journey to understanding these concepts began at the age of 16, when I first became captivated by physical fitness, nutrition, and personal development.

I still treasure the hardcover Reader's Digest book, *Eat Better, Live Better: A South African Guide to Nutrition and Good Health*, which I acquired during my early high school years. It was my companion in studying Home Economics, a subject that ignited my passion for wellness. Little did I know that this interest in nutrition and well-being would later shape the course of my life. In my late 20s, it led me to make one of the biggest decisions and accomplishments of my life—launching a career in the wellness industry. I truly believe that my Home Economics teacher, Mrs. Henry, and that book laid the foundation for my enduring passion: the belief that our health is our wealth.

As my journey in wellness evolved, and through the wisdom gained from my business endeavors, podcast, growth in my faith, and personal life experiences, I've come to realize that true health, wealth, and being 'fit for life' are not just about our daily step count, vegetable intake, sleep quality, or even the size of our bank accounts. While these factors are important, they are only part of the picture. Health and wealth, in their truest sense, are multifaceted concepts. I have come to realise that at the heart of it all lies the inner nurturing of our spiritual selves.

## The Foundation of True Wellness

When I think about health being our wealth, I think of self-care—shining a spotlight on our spiritual, mental, physical, and emotional well-being. It's about taking the steps to live a life full of purpose, joy, peace, clarity, hope, love, and, above all, faith. That's what it means to glow from the inside out and be truly fit for life.

In my early years as a Personal and Group Fitness Trainer, I would often ask people what the phrase "Your health is your wealth" meant to them. Most would immediately think of physical health—being fit, eating well, and having the energy and longevity to enjoy life. Some would connect it to financial success—luxurious vacations, designer clothes, and the ability to enjoy the fruits of their labour. After all, society often equates wealth with success, both in accomplishments and in financial strength.

Sadly, in today's world, we can sometimes get caught up in chasing external markers of success—designer handbags, flashy cars, or a picture-perfect life curated for social media. While these things may offer fleeting happiness, I have discovered they cannot provide the deep-rooted joy and fulfillment that comes from within and what our spirit longs for.

This resonates so profoundly with me because, for so long, I chased happiness—believing it would bring peace and contentment, no matter the circumstances. But I clung to the wrong things, the external markers society promised would lead to lasting joy. I was wrong and misled. Despite my achievements, I still felt an aching longing for something more: peace, joy, clarity, and stability.

## Steps to Glow from the Inside Out

In my contribution to the anthology, *She Stands Strong: 30 Personal Stories of Strength and Resilience*, I shared part of my journey—my childhood and early adulthood, a time marked by fear, doubt, change, and emotional struggle. Back then, I was disconnected from my true self.

I was like a boat without a rudder, taking guidance from all the wrong places. That disconnection continued into my early fifties, but today, I finally know I have found the right path, taking daily steps with God as my foundation, my source of guidance and strength. Today, my faith supports me in moving beyond what once held me back.

So, what simple steps can you take today to begin your own journey of glowing from the inside out and becoming truly 'fit for life'? Here are three essential practices to consider incorporating into your daily life—simple yet powerful steps that will help you connect with your inner well-being and become a beacon of light for others.

## Step One: Rooted in Spiritual Wellness

Our spiritual well-being is the cornerstone of our true inner glow. It nurtures our connection to God—or, for some, a higher power—and provides us with a deeper sense of purpose that sustains us through life's challenges. When we nurture our spiritual selves through prayer, worship, and quiet moments of reflection, connecting with like-minded communities, we cultivate a deep well of hope, peace, joy, strength, and resilience.

This connection allows us to face life's difficulties with grace, knowing that we are never alone. Personally, I believe in God's divine guidance, offering wisdom, support, and love. Trusting this guidance has given me unshakable strength, peace, and joy, along with healing, knowing that no matter what I face, I am supported and capable of shining through.

## Step Two: Mind over Matter

Mental wellness is equally essential to glowing from the inside out. Our mindset shapes how we navigate life's challenges, how we perceive ourselves, and how we see the world around us. A positive mindset helps fuel emotional resilience and strengthens our overall well-being. Practices such as daily affirmations, mindfulness, and consciously choosing positivity can shift our perspective, clearing space for peace and joy to take deep roots.

In the chapter *She Stands Strong*, I shared how making friends with fear and doubt is a mindset shift and has been transformative for me. Instead of avoiding these uncomfortable emotions, I learned to embrace them. This mindset shift opened the door to profound personal growth and allowed me to move toward joy and inner peace.

## Step Three: Honouring your Body

To glow from the inside out, we must also honour our physical health. Our bodies are not just vessels; they are an integral part of our well-being. When we care for our bodies—as God wants us to through exercise, mindful eating, and prioritizing sleep—we create a solid foundation that supports our spiritual peace and mental clarity.

Our physical health is deeply intertwined with our spiritual and emotional well-being. By viewing our bodies with gratitude and care, it becomes a reflection of the inner glow we've nurtured in spirit and mind. Regular physical activity, healthy food sources, and restful sleep are powerful ways to cultivate joy and vitality.

## Embrace Your Inner Glow

To glow from the inside out is to connect with your core being—your spirit—and to ground yourself in peace, joy, and purpose. It's about choosing to nurture and radiate that energy into the world. When we align our lives with our spiritual health first, we naturally begin to shine brighter.

As you begin to cultivate your own inner glow, remember that you are not just taking care of yourself—you are also becoming a light for others. Your radiance can inspire those around you, offering them the strength to embark on their own journeys of self-care and wellness.

I encourage you to reflect on these steps and start with one small action today. Whether it's beginning a regular prayer routine, practicing daily affirmations, keeping a gratitude journal, connecting with like-minded communities, or taking regular walks in nature to nurture your spirit by connecting with its beauty—honouring the true essence of who you are with each small step will bring you closer to the radiant person you were always meant to be.

Join me on my podcast *Beyond to Freedom* to discover practical steps for moving beyond whatever holds you back and begin to 'glow from the inside out'.

#yougotthis

## Tammy Dungan

Founder of Limitless Ladies Network LLC
Wellness Coach

https://www.linkedin.com/company/limitless-ladies-network-llc/
https://www.facebook.com/people/Limitless-Ladies-Network/61566008245164/
https://limitlessladiesnetwork.com/

After nearly 20 years of facilitating corporate trainings, conferences, and workshops at tech start-ups, Tammy left the industry in 2019 to launch a mobile stand-up paddleboard business. Shortly thereafter she was diagnosed with Lyme Disease and Spondyloarthritis. For three years she struggled to balance work, home and her autoimmune symptoms that landed herself in a wheelchair. Frustrated and driven to make changes, she educated herself through wellness courses, literature, and research to implement holistic lifestyle adjustments to successfully regain her strength, mobility, and well-being. Her struggles fueled her passion to serve women suffering from similar afflictions. The Limitless Ladies Network was launched in 2024 to empower the ladies to advocate for themselves and embrace a journey of holistic self-care. She is also a Board Member of the Soroptimist International of Willimantic as an avid advocate for education for women and young girls to thrive.

# A Holistic Journey - From Lame to Limitless

By Tammy Dungan

Empowerment: "the state of being empowered to do something: the power, right, or authority to do something."[1]

I have always been a driven woman who wanted to succeed in life. At the age of 45, I finally felt like I was "successful," having worked my way up to a senior-level position and on the management team at a tech startup. However, I quickly learned that success without purpose isn't really success. Rising to the top meant lots of sacrifices that required long hours, lots of travel, high stress, and precious time away from my family. So, although it appeared that I had finally achieved my goal of being a senior executive with a small team, the travel, stress, and anxiety, led to a lack of self-care that was not sustainable.

Just months before COVID, I decided to quit my full-time job and start a mobile stand-up paddleboard business with my husband so I could spend more time with my kids. Jumping headfirst into a very physical profession after sitting 12 to 14 hours a day without any exercise or self-care quickly took a toll on my body. Within just a couple of months, I injured myself with three herniated discs from lifting 10–12-foot paddle boards and paddling long distances on group tours.

Determined to finish out the season, I kept moving forward with the help of my husband and kids. However, my back injuries compounded my health matters as I soon began having uncontrollable swelling and pain in my knees and ankles, making it very difficult to walk. The swelling got so bad that I was forced to use a wheelchair during our family vacation to Disney: although the kids immensely enjoyed the benefits of my new handicap status with first-in-line access to all the

---

[1] https://www.merriam-webster.com/dictionary/empowerment

rides. As the months went on, my body felt as though it was slowly rejecting itself. I woke up in tears every morning after just a few hours of restless and painful sleep, dreading the two flights of stairs that I would have to slide down on my bum in order to eat my breakfast.

In the off-season, I was finally able to focus my attention on my own self-care. I began seeking the expertise of several medical professionals and specialists as my symptoms increasingly got worse with each day that passed. As I made my way through multiple X-rays, MRIs, and CT scans with multiple medical specialists for my aches, pains, and swelling in my back, knee, and ankle, I was constantly told that although there might be a slight issue, there was nothing that could be done. No surgery was needed or even suggested treatments, other than pills to help with the pain. I left each appointment feeling hopeless and discouraged, like it was all in my head. Yet every day, I was in agonizing pain and experiencing uncontrollable swelling to my left side by the end of the day. As exhausted as I was, I could not sleep. The pain was unbearable 24/7, and at my lowest point, I was begging for my life to be over.

Six months into my journey for truth, I was diagnosed with three types of Lyme disease, and a few months later, I was diagnosed with spondyloarthritis,[2] a group term for inflammatory diseases that cause joint pain and/or arthritis—a very painful form of arthritis. Although I did not have the worst case where the body becomes almost mummified, it sure did feel as though it was getting to that point when one morning, I could not open my mouth wide enough to eat breakfast.

It was somewhat comforting to have answers for my constant agony but frustrated by the treatment options outlined with about five different pills to control the pain and swelling and that long-term use may cause major side effects such as cancer and other life-threatening diseases. This treatment plan was unacceptable to me. I was not going to just accept

---

[2] https://www.healthline.com/health/spondyloarthritis

the fact that at my young age, I would have to painfully suffer for the rest of my life and take pills to cope.

My diagnosis **empowered** me to take charge of my life and advocate even harder for my health and well-being. I decided I would NOT resort to taking pills with deadly side effects as the solution to my situation. I began feverishly reading, researching, and learning all that I could about spondyloarthritis and Lyme disease. I started to journal about what I was putting into my body and how it was affecting me each day. As you can imagine, my mental state was in a bad place and needed an overhaul. I incorporated new routines like five-minute morning meditations, gentle at-home yoga, and nightly journaling to improve my outlook and reduce anxiety and stress. My health team soon expanded beyond traditional medical doctors to include a good physical therapist, chiropractor, and bioenergetic holistic practitioner who together helped me through the pain and provided sound advice for each new specialist I was referred to.

Life's struggles can empower us to own our health and have self-advocacy. If you don't care for or advocate for yourself, who will? With this motto in mind, I became immersed in learning all I could about how the body reacts to stress, foods, toxins, pathogens, and lack of sleep. It was uplifting and empowering to know that good quality health was within my control.

My unfortunate health issues profoundly changed my life. I am a life-long learner, educator, and advocate for women's health. I believe that all women can take control of their health to improve their lives and thrive, not just survive. That is why I became a Certified Autoimmune Holistic Nutrition Specialist and started the Limitless Ladies Network LLC. My mission is to provide valuable resources and educate women on how they, too, can thrive, not just survive. I am so grateful that I believed in myself enough to prioritize self-care so others can learn from my challenges and be empowered to live their best life too.

Through my journey with holistic healthcare practitioners and my own self-exploration of diet and lifestyle adjustments, I was able to heal my body from within and reverse the effects of spondyloarthritis and Lyme disease. Upon discharge of services from my rheumatologist, he expressed his awe and shock that I was able to be released without pain, swelling, or discomfort, completely off all prescription medications. That day was one of the best days of my life. I left his office glowing with pride for investing in myself and advocating for my health and well-being. It is my mission to coach, educate, empower, and advocate for all women suffering unnecessarily so they, too, can thrive.

Connect with me at:
thrive@limitlessladiesnetwork.com

Sign up for our newsletter:
https://limitlessladiesnetwork.com/sign-up

Follow us on Facebook:
https://www.facebook.com/people/Limitless-Ladies-Network/61566008245164/

Follow us on YouTube:
https://www.youtube.com/@LimitlessLadiesNetwork-2thrive

## Tishana Eason Meyers

Owner of Brooklyn Beauty Bar
Self Love Coach

https://www.linkedin.com/in/tishana-eason-92912761/
https://www.facebook.com/BrooklynstylistTishana
https://www.instagram.com/coachbrooklynselfhealing/
https://brooklynbeautybarga.com/

Tishana also known as Brooklyn was born and raised in Brooklyn, New York. Her parents came from Panama in search of the American dream to provide for her and her siblings. They always told her that education was very important. Wanting the best for her they put her in one of the top schools in Brooklyn. She attended Bishop Loughlin Memorial High School. At the age of 19 years old, she became a salon owner. This is where she began to counsel women behind the chair. Once Brooklyn became a wife to a military spouse and a mother, she put her career on hold. She understood that her spouse's career was very demanding and her children needed her more. 37 years of age was a turning point for Brooklyn. Life as she knew it changed. She was now separated from her husband and on her own with two kids. Georgia became her state of residency. This was a fresh new start for her and the kids. She made the best of her situation and overcame the storms that came her way. Before you knew it Brooklyn opened a salon, started a fashion line business and took her life experience, and became a life coach.

# She Glows from the Darkness

By Tishana Eason Meyers

They can see your glow and miss your struggles. Life, as it seems, hasn't been easy for me. It has been a rough journey. A journey that left me to question God, "Why me?" or "Have I done something wrong?" I'm here to give my truth, hoping to encourage others who may feel like just giving up or don't know where to begin showing up for themselves. Also, to know that you, too, can glow from your darkness. Let's make the changes now. Not prioritizing yourself can stunt your growth in every area of your life. One wouldn't think this could have an impact on one's life, but it does. Once I started putting in the work, not just talking and thinking about it—changing my mindset—that's when I began to glow in my own skin. This is when I discovered her, and she is me: the entrepreneur, life coach, fashion designer, hairstylist/salon owner. The makeover queen—that is what they call me. I had so much inside of me that couldn't come alive until I started loving myself. According to God's words, "I'm fearfully and wonderfully made." If I only believed that. These were just words to me at one point in my life with no real meaning. It all started from my childhood. Growing up in Brooklyn, New York, gives you this aura of confidence and this tough attitude. Really suppressing your feelings. So, is it genuine confidence? Or is it just a façade? Most people are hiding behind something. Think about that, what are you hiding behind? Because it shows up through our actions. Being truthful with yourself can really transform your life. I had to learn the hard way.

I grew up seeing my mother putting her husband and her children first. She never seemed to relax. She worked two jobs to make ends meet. So, learning self-care and self-love at a young age didn't exist for me. As a grown woman, I realize what we do in front of our children sets the tone for them, and that's why "I married my father." My ex-husband was a very familiar place for me. I just felt safe from what I knew but not thinking about what was good for me. The red flags were in my face, and I pretended to be color blind, not seeing red but pink. I had to suffer the consequences of not loving myself. I was very young and, let's face it, I didn't have any standards. In a Panamanian household, you don't talk about relationships or sex. Education is everything, which is beautiful, but when you don't talk to your children about life, let them know they're worthy, and encourage them to have high standards for themselves, they will settle for anything. I was one of those children. I was impressed by my ex-husband's career path, so his behavior received a pass. Sad to say but this is how I handled business and other areas in my life. I would tell myself I was the problem. Falling deeper and deeper into depression because of the poison I was feeding myself. I found myself living in the shadow of my husband's career, no more setting goals for myself. It was very hard when we had to move every three years because he was in the military. I had three small children who needed me because of his deployments. I was struggling mentally and financially. I was emotionally a mess. I decided to journal my thoughts throughout the marriage, and it gave me an escape from the cheating and the narcissistic behavior I was receiving from my ex-husband.

If you're going through a rough time at this present moment in your life, STOP right now and get yourself a journal. It saved my life. I was busy pointing the finger at my ex but not realizing my own self-abuse. I was able to look back at my behavior in the journals and how my children were being affected by my lack of self-love and self-care. One day, I woke up and didn't like what I saw in the mirror. I decided to leave the marriage and invest in my future. I didn't know how I was going to do it; however, it was a risk I was willing to take.

I know, I know, sounds really good, right? I must be real, I was scared. I went back. I tried to make the marriage work, not knowing I was being gaslit. I thought he loved me and didn't want to lose me. Boy, was I wrong. It took him little time to treat me even worse than before. I went to therapy to start putting in the work. I had to change my mindset on how I looked at myself. I didn't see myself the way God saw me. That was my biggest problem. People would treat you the way you treat yourself. Take a moment and live in your truth. Are you showing yourself self-love? One must know the true meaning in order to GLOW. Self-love is having a high regard for your own well-being and happiness. Taking care of your own needs and not sacrificing your well-being to please others. When I looked up the true meaning, it was a turning point for me. I wanted to walk in my true calling. This meant healing, inner peace, and living my dreams. Say with me, "I will put myself first. I can't pour into anyone's cup if mine is empty. I will make time for myself. I will not be a people pleaser."

These are things I said to myself every day and still do.

I put my dreams and career on hold for years. Not anymore. I put my trust in God, and I opened Brooklyn Beauty Bar salon with only five thousand dollars. That was all I had in the bank. I was determined to make it work. Before I knew it, I was able to take care of my kids financially. I went from a salon to creating my own clothing line, to being a life coach to help women like me. That journal I began to write while I was married is now a book, *Living His Lie, but Found the Truth*. See, self-love turned into healing, and healing produced a glow from my darkness. The light just gets brighter and brighter. So, you got this. Glow, Glow, Glow. Don't hold your story to yourself; it will help others to Glow.

## Sonia Rodrigues

Transition to Wellness
Psychotherapist & Life Transition Coach

https://www.linkedin.com/in/sonia-rodrigues-48b87149/
https://www.facebook.com/SoniaRodriguesLPC/
https://instagram.com/transition.to.wellness
http://www.transitiontowellness.com/
https://soniarodrigues-marto.tribesites.com/

Sonia Rodrigues has been a licensed psychotherapist for over 20 years. She is the owner of a psychotherapy and coaching practice called Transition to Wellness. She has worked with people of all ages, helping them navigate various challenges in their life. She utilizes a holistic approach and provides a safe and supportive environment where her clients can feel supported on their path towards healing from their traumatic experiences and guided towards creating the life they desire. She provides individual therapy, coaching and also offers a variety of workshops on topics related to trauma, post-traumatic growth and fostering resilience.

# Reclaiming My Power:
# A Journey of Healing and Growth

By Sonia Rodrigues

Reclaiming your well-being carries a quiet strength, a gentle yet powerful glow that shines from within when you nurture your body, mind, and spirit. This is the true essence of wellness, and this chapter is here to guide you in accessing that vibrant energy. As a working mother of three, I know how challenging it is to find any time for yourself. It is a struggle I know. As a holistic psychotherapist who has walked my own path of healing, I want to share with you the profound transformation that can occur when we embrace the holistic approach to health and truly take care of ourselves personally, professionally and spiritually.

## SHE GLOWS: Empowering Women Through Wellness and Self-Care

Self-care isn't just about bubble baths and face masks—though those can certainly be part of the process. True wellness is about living in alignment with who you are and nurturing yourself in a way that reflects your innate value. It is about creating space for healing, growth, and joy amidst the demands of everyday life.

In this chapter, we will explore the transformative power of wellness. Together, we will unpack how to nourish your body, mind, and soul. We will dive into the practical tools and holistic practices that will allow you to ignite your inner glow, just as I did, in my own healing journey.

Self-care is not a luxury, but a vital practice that allows us to show up fully for ourselves and the world around us. It is about cultivating a deep sense of self-worth, setting boundaries that protect your energy, and embracing habits that nurture your mental, emotional, and physical well-being. By prioritizing self-care, we learn to honor our needs and desires, creating a foundation of strength from which we can thrive. Integrating self-care practices into your daily routine can enhance your well-being and also empower you to live a life that truly reflects your fullest potential.

## The Elements of Wellness

One of the most powerful elements of wellness is recognizing that you are not alone in your struggles or triumphs. As women, we are often taught to be caretakers, to put others first, and to neglect our own needs. Yet the truth is, we cannot fully nurture others if we are not nurturing ourselves. We must also recognize the importance of modeling the behavior of taking care of ourselves for those around us, especially our children, because we want them to learn early on that taking care of ourselves is the foundation to achieving mind/body wellness.

Another key element of wellness is the practice of connection, not only with ourselves but with others who support and uplift us. Building a community of like-minded individuals who prioritize wellness creates a powerful network of encouragement and accountability. Whether it is through close friendships, family, or support groups, surrounding ourselves with people who value self-care helps reinforce the message that taking care of our well-being is an essential part of our lives. By fostering these connections, we remind ourselves that we are part of a greater collective, and in nourishing each other, we strengthen the foundation of wellness for everyone.

## Practical Tips: Actionable Steps to Incorporate Wellness Strategies Into Your Life

While many of us may have some ideas about what wellness strategies look like, we often struggle to identify all of the ways in which we can incorporate it into our lives. Here are some practical, actionable steps you can incorporate into your daily routine to begin nurturing your body and mind:

1. **Mindfulness Practices:** Mindfulness is about being present in the moment and listening to your body's cues. Begin by setting aside just five minutes each day to focus on your breath. Close your eyes, breathe deeply, and check in with yourself. What is your body telling you? Are you tense? Tired? Anxious? By practicing mindfulness, you can better manage stress, reduce anxiety, and make more intentional choices about your well-being.

2. **Nutrition for Nourishment:** We all know that what we eat affects how we feel, but many of us still neglect the importance of a balanced, nourishing diet. Start by incorporating whole foods into your meals—fruits, vegetables, healthy fats, and lean proteins. Hydration is equally crucial, so drink plenty of water throughout the day. If you struggle with what to eat, try focusing on eating foods that make you feel energized and balanced, not foods that simply fill a void.

3. **Beauty Rituals with a Purpose:** Beauty rituals aren't just about enhancing your outer appearance—they're about creating moments of care and connection with yourself. Take time to pamper your skin, treat yourself to a nourishing face mask, or indulge in a calming bath. These small rituals are opportunities to slow down, tune in to your body, and celebrate your uniqueness.

4. **Fitness: Move with Intention:** Physical activity doesn't have to mean grueling workouts at the gym. Instead, find an activity that brings you joy—whether it's yoga, dancing, walking in nature, or swimming. Fitness is about honoring your body's need for movement and strength, not about achieving a specific aesthetic. When you move with intention, you'll feel more grounded, energized, and connected to your body.

5. **Start a Daily Gratitude Practice:** One of the simplest yet most powerful wellness practices is cultivating gratitude. Each day, take a moment to reflect on the things you're thankful for—big or small. Whether you write them down in a journal, say them aloud, or simply reflect on them in your mind, acknowledging what you're grateful for shifts your focus toward positivity and abundance. This practice helps reduce stress, enhances mental clarity, and strengthens your emotional well-being by reminding you of the good in your life. By starting and ending your day with gratitude, you create a positive mindset that supports your overall wellness journey.

6. **Reconnect with Activities That Bring You Joy:** Make time for the things that light you up—whether it's dancing, painting, playing music, or engaging in sports. These activities, which nourish your creative spirit and physical body, are vital to your emotional and mental health. Reconnecting with your passions allows you to express yourself freely and experience joy in the present moment. Whether you take a dance class, play your favorite instrument, or simply enjoy a walk in nature, these activities serve as reminders of the things that truly bring you happiness and fulfillment. Make space for them regularly to enhance your sense of well-being and keep you connected to what you love.

## Achieving Balance and Nourishing Your Mind, Body, and Spirit

As a psychotherapist, I have found that achieving balance and nourishing your mind, body, and spirit are essential for overall well-being. Through my own practice, I have come to understand the importance of integrating self-care in a way that aligns with your physical, emotional, and mental health. Here are a few key insights that I have found to be particularly valuable:

- **Nourishing Your Body:** It's important to focus on balance, not restriction, when it comes to nutrition. Nourishing your body with whole, nutrient-dense foods does more than just fuel your physical self—it has a profound impact on your emotional and mental well-being as well. When you eat with intention, you're also nurturing your spirit, creating a foundation for health that supports your overall vitality and resilience.

- **Listening to Your Body:** Fitness isn't about perfection; it's about listening to what your body needs and finding a rhythm that supports your lifestyle. It's easy to get caught up in the idea that exercise must be intense to be effective, but even small, consistent practices—like a daily stretching routine—can have a tremendous impact on your energy levels and emotional state. The goal is to connect with your body in a way that feels supportive, not overwhelming.

- **Cultivating Self-Compassion:** One of the most essential elements of mental and emotional well-being is self-compassion. Healing and personal growth are processes that take time, and it's important to treat yourself with patience and kindness along the way. I often remind my clients that growth doesn't happen overnight, and taking time for self-reflection is key to developing a compassionate inner dialogue that fosters emotional resilience. The journey of healing is ongoing, and embracing self-compassion helps you navigate it with grace and understanding.

By integrating these practices into your daily life, you can create a holistic approach to wellness that supports not only your body but also your mind and spirit.

Wellness is an integrated experience where each part of you is connected. To truly thrive, we must address all aspects of our being: body, mind, and spirit. Here are some holistic approaches to help you nurture yourself:

- **Meditation:** Regular meditation helps reduce stress, improve focus, and cultivate a sense of peace. You can start with simple breathing techniques or guided meditations. Over time, you'll find that your ability to handle challenges with calm and clarity increases.

- **Aromatherapy:** Essential oils can have a powerful impact on your emotional well-being. Lavender is known for its calming properties, while citrus oils like lemon or orange can uplift your mood. Create a ritual of diffusing calming scents in your home or use them during a relaxing bath or meditation.

- **Yoga:** Yoga offers not only physical benefits but also mental and emotional healing. Through mindful movement and breathwork, you can release tension and reconnect with your body. Whether you're new to yoga or experienced, there's always a deeper layer of healing to uncover.

## Empowerment Tools: Boosting Self-Esteem and Setting Boundaries

As you embark on your journey of wellness, it is essential to embrace empowerment tools that support your growth. Setting healthy boundaries is a powerful act of self-care. It is okay to say no when something doesn't serve you or when your energy is being drained by external demands. Reclaim your power by honoring your needs and aspirations.

Additionally, boosting your self-esteem is vital for wellness. Practice affirmations daily, remind yourself of your worth, and surround yourself with people who uplift and support you. As you strengthen your sense of self, you'll discover a new well of confidence and vitality.

Positive affirmations can be a powerful tool for reshaping our mindset and fostering positive change. By repeating positive statements about ourselves, we can rewire our thought patterns, replacing self-doubt and negativity with confidence and self-worth. These simple yet profound statements help to cultivate a mindset of possibility, encouraging us to believe in our potential and take empowered actions. When practiced consistently, affirmations can serve as a daily reminder of our strengths, helping to build resilience and reinforce the belief that we are capable of overcoming challenges and creating the life we desire.

## Conclusion: Embracing Your Inner Glow

The journey to wellness is a continuous, evolving process, not a straight line. It's about reconnecting with yourself, nurturing your body and mind, and living a life filled with vitality, joy, and love. By incorporating small acts of self-care into your daily routine and embracing holistic practices, you can ignite your inner glow and reclaim your power. Remember, you are worthy of care, rest, and joy, and every small step you take toward healing matters.

Healing is a lifelong journey that requires patience, resilience, and self-compassion. It's a process of growth, and as you continue, you'll discover that you are stronger than you ever imagined. You have the power within you to rise above challenges and transform your life. Trust in your strength, embrace your power, and step into the radiant, resilient person you are becoming.

As you move forward on your path, remember that healing and growth are about progress, not perfection. Celebrate the small victories and the lessons learned along the way, for each step is a testament to your resilience and courage. Trust that the journey you are on is unfolding exactly as it is meant to and that the power to shape your future lies within you. Embrace each moment with compassion for yourself, knowing that you are always worthy of the care, love, and attention you give to others. You have everything you need within you to shine brightly and create a life filled with meaning and purpose. Keep moving forward with faith in yourself and your ability to reclaim your power and to creating a life that reflects your true brilliance and potential.

## Dr. Josette Ga-an

Founder of Dr Sleep Solutions

https://www.facebook.com/josette.gaan
https://www.instagram.com/the_options_ph/
https://drsleepsolutions.com
https://drgaan.carrd.co

Dr. Josette Ga-an is a board-certified dentist specializing in Airway Dentistry, Myofunctional Orthodontics, and Dental Sleep Medicine. She holds a Bachelor's degree in Biology and is a U.S.-certified Sleep Science Coach. With a passion for bridging oral health and overall wellness, Dr. Ga-an founded Dr. Sleep Solutions to empower patients to achieve better sleep and health through innovative dental and sleep strategies. She also created the Early Airway Training Program (EAT Pro) for her young patients, promoting lifelong healthy breathing and sleep habits. Beyond her clinical practice, Dr. Ga-an is an advocate for sleep education, leading community initiatives that emphasize the vital connection between breathing and sleep. In her leisure time, Dr. Ga-an enjoys calligraphy and exploring sleep-friendly destinations, blending creativity and wellness into every aspect of her life and work.

# Why Am I Still Tired? The Sleep Secret That Changed Everything

By Dr. Josette Ga-an

## The Frustration of Feeling Exhausted After Eight Hours of Sleep

Anna sat across from me, her shoulders slumped, eyes heavy with exhaustion. She had been following all the "rules." Eight hours of sleep every night. No caffeine after noon. Yet, every morning she woke up feeling just as drained as when she went to bed. She was frustrated, confused, and, honestly, a little desperate.

"I don't understand it, Dr. Josette," she said, shaking her head. "I'm doing everything right. I sleep for eight hours every night, but I feel exhausted all the time. Something's not right, but I don't know what."

I could see the toll this was taking on her: a constant cycle of fatigue that no amount of rest seemed to fix. After hearing her story, I asked her about her **sleep patterns**, her **breathing**, and how she felt during the day. What I learned next would unlock the missing piece to her puzzle.

The Missing Piece: Mouth Breathing and Its Impact on Sleep

When I asked Anna how she breathed during the night, she mentioned that she'd been a **mouth breather** for as long as she could remember. This detail was crucial. Mouth breathing, especially during sleep, can cause a range of issues, from **disrupted sleep cycles** to poor oxygenation of the body. It's no wonder that even after eight hours of sleep, Anna wasn't feeling rested.

I told her that **breathing properly**—especially through the nose—during both the day and the night, plays a huge role in the **quality of sleep** we get. Our bodies need **deep, restorative sleep**, but that can't happen if we're not breathing correctly. I introduced Anna to **diaphragmatic breathing** (or deep belly breathing) to help reset her breathing pattern and bring more oxygen into her system during the day.

A Simple Breathing Exercise for Better Sleep:

**1. Sit or Lie Down Comfortably:**
Find a relaxing position where you feel supported.

**2. Place One Hand on Your Chest, and One on Your Belly:**
This will help you feel where the air is moving in your body.

**3. Inhale Slowly Through Your Nose for Four Seconds:**
Let the air fill your lungs deeply, allowing your belly to rise (not your chest).

**4. Hold for a Moment:**
Take a short pause before exhaling.

**5. Exhale Slowly Through Your Nose for Six Seconds:**
Slowly release the breath, feeling your belly gently deflate.

**6. Repeat for Five Minutes Daily:**
By practicing this simple technique, you activate your **parasympathetic nervous system**, signaling your body to relax, reduce stress, and prepare for better sleep.

## Tongue Posture Training: A Simple Habit with Big Results

Along with proper breathing, I introduced Anna to another game-changing habit: **tongue posture**. I explained that the position of your tongue during the day can affect how well you breathe at night.

The goal was to help Anna keep her **tongue resting on the roof of her mouth** rather than letting it drop down or rest against her teeth. This subtle shift would promote **nasal breathing**, which is far more beneficial than mouth breathing for both daytime energy and sleep quality.

**How to Practice Proper Tongue Posture:**

**1. Place the Tip of Your Tongue on the Roof of Your Mouth:**
The tip should rest just behind your front teeth, with the rest of your tongue gently touching the roof of your mouth.

**2. Keep Your Teeth Slightly Apart:**
Let your teeth relax and stay naturally separated.

**3. Keep Your Lips Closed Gently:**
Your lips should be closed without tension or force.

**4. Breathe Through Your Nose:**
Focus on keeping your breath **through the nose** during the day, which helps keep the airway clear and promotes better sleep.

## The Importance of Sun Exposure for Better Sleep

In addition to improving her breathing and tongue posture, I also recommended that Anna get **sun exposure** early in the morning. Natural sunlight helps regulate the body's **circadian rhythm**, which plays a major role in sleep quality. By getting sunlight exposure in the morning, the body receives the signal to release **serotonin** and prepare for a restful night.

I encouraged Anna to spend at least **10–15 minutes outside** in the morning light, even if it was just to sit by the window with her coffee. This would help reset her internal clock, leading to better sleep at night and more energy during the day.

## A Surprising Transformation: From Exhausted to Energized

Just two weeks later, Anna came back to my office, beaming with a newfound sense of energy. "I can't believe it," she said, "I'm actually feeling better. I've been practicing the breathing exercises, focusing on my tongue posture, and getting morning sunlight, and I'm waking up feeling more refreshed than I have in years."

By paying attention to her **breathing habits**, improving her **tongue posture**, and getting **morning sun exposure**, Anna had transformed her sleep from merely "sleeping" to **restorative sleep**. She was finally getting the rest she needed to feel truly energized throughout the day.

## The Secret to True Rest

If you find yourself feeling tired despite getting enough sleep, it might be time to consider these simple practices. They could be the missing link to waking up truly refreshed.

So, take a moment. Try the breathing exercises, focus on your tongue posture, and soak up a little sunlight. The next time you wake up, you might just find yourself smiling because you've unlocked the key to not just surviving the day—but thriving.

Remember: True wellness comes when you listen to your body, treat it with kindness, and provide it with the tools it needs to shine.

Here's to the glow that starts from within—and it doesn't take a beauty routine to get there.

## Amie Rich

Amie Rich Coaching
Life Coach and Spiritual Hypnotherapist

https://www.facebook.com/profile.php?id=100094152004634
https://www.instagram.com/awakenedwithamie/
https://amierich.com/
https://amierichcoaching.com/

Amie Rich is a certified life coach, spiritual hypnotherapist, and energy healer passionate about empowering women to prioritize themselves and embrace their self-worth. With over 28 years of corporate experience, Amie understands the challenges of balancing life's demands while navigating personal growth. Her healing journey began with a desire to break free from people-pleasing tendencies, leading her to explore energy healing, life coaching, Reiki, and holistic wellness. As the author of The ABCs of Self-Love and a contributor to the upcoming book She Grows Stronger, Amie shares personal stories and practical tools to inspire transformation. She also offers a variety of resources, including guided meditations, workshops, and coaching sessions, to help others unlock their potential.

# Igniting Your Inner Light
## Self-Love as the Foundation of Healing

By Amie Rich

Let's start with a confession—I'm a recovering people-pleaser. For years, dare I say decades, my life was like a never-ending game of "How can I make everyone happy and completely ignore myself?" Spoiler alert: I lost that game—big time. But losing it was the best thing that ever happened to me, because it led me here, to this beautiful journey of self-love and healing.

Hi, I'm Amie Rich—a certified empowerment coach, and spiritual hypnotherapist. I've dedicated my life to helping women discover the transformative power of self-love because I've lived the journey myself. For years, I wore the masks of corporate success, a "perfect" mom, and a people-pleaser, but underneath it all, I was exhausted, lonely, and disconnected from my true authentic self. Learning to embrace self-love not only transformed my life but also became the foundation of my healing and the work I now share with others.

## The Turning Point—Choosing Myself

My journey to self-love wasn't a smooth road. It began at a crossroads, facing the pain of feeling invisible in my own life. The breaking point came when I realized that my constant people-pleasing, perfectionism, and fear of disappointing others were draining me completely. My marriage was not healthy, and I decided to get a divorce—a decision that terrified me to my core but was rooted in love for myself and my children. I had spent so long trying to be everything to everyone that I didn't even know who I was anymore.

As a single parent, I struggled with loneliness, the guilt of not being able to give my kids everything, and the fear of failing them. But what I learned was life-changing: I couldn't pour from an empty cup. I had to choose myself, not just for me but to show my children what it looks like to honor your own worth.

## The Power of Embracing Self-Love

So, self-love became my guiding light, and as I embraced it, I discovered the incredible healing power of energy work. These tools helped me release the pain of old wounds and limiting beliefs, clearing the emotional blocks that had kept me stuck for so long. Through many healing practices, I felt myself realign with the person I was always meant to be—strong, whole, and empowered.

Equally transformative was developing a consistent self-care routine. I started a routine, and to this day still begin each morning with meditation, allowing myself to start the day from a place of calm and clarity. Journaling became a trusted companion, giving me a safe space to explore my emotions, set intentions, and reflect on my growth. These daily rituals grounded me, reminding me that self-love is cultivated in the small, intentional moments we carve out for ourselves.

Embracing self-love also gave me the courage to re-enter the dating world. It wasn't about finding someone to complete me but about stepping into my worth and trusting divine timing. Eventually, I met my twin flame, who is now my husband. Together, we built a partnership that is rooted in mutual respect and love—a reflection of the love I learned to give myself first.

## The Ripple Effect of Self-Love

When you embrace self-love, you tap into your own power, and that power ripples into every area of your life. For me, it meant discovering that I had a voice and a message to share. I realized that self-love isn't just the foundation of my own healing but of all healing. And healing, at its core, is a self-driven journey, though it's one that's made brighter with the guidance of others who believe in you.

Through my work as a coach and hypnotherapist, I've had the privilege of helping women recognize that empowerment is within their reach. Self-love is not a destination—it's a journey that begins with a single step: choosing yourself. When you do, you'll find that everything else—healing, confidence, and even your dreams—begins to fall into place.

## A Glow That Never Fades

Self-love isn't about achieving perfection; it's about honoring who you are in this moment. It's about saying no to what drains you and yes to what fills your soul. It's about recognizing that your glow comes from within and letting it light your path forward.

So, here's my challenge to you: take that first step today. Look in the mirror and acknowledge the incredible person staring back at you. For me, I wrote a simple yet powerful message on my mirror to greet my beautiful face every single morning: *I am enough*. Seeing those words every day became a ritual of self-affirmation, a daily reminder of my worth and strength.

I invite you to do the same. Write your own empowering message on your mirror—something that speaks to your heart and lifts your spirit. Let it be the first thing you see in the morning and the last thing you see at night. These small acts of self-love can transform the way you see yourself and the life you create.

Remember, self-love isn't a luxury; it's your birthright. And when you embrace self-love, you are stepping into your power and embodying the essence of *She Glows*. You have the ability to heal, grow, and thrive—and your journey lights the way for others to do the same. Together, we create a world where every woman's glow contributes to a brighter, more empowered future.

Dear friend, your inner light is waiting to shine. When you choose to love yourself—truly, deeply, unapologetically—you ignite a power that transforms not just your life but the lives of everyone around you. Healing begins with self-love, and I am here to guide you on that journey.

If you are looking for a spiritual cheerleader, I am here for you. You can find me at www.amierich.com or on Instagram at @awakenedwithamie, where I share resources, tools, and guidance to help you thrive. Let's ignite your inner light together—you deserve to glow.

## Dr. Nefertiti S Fisher

CEO of Beautiful One Inc.

https://www.linkedin.com/in/nefertitifisher/
https://www.facebook.com/profile.php?id=100000168393655
https://www.instagram.com/icome2inspireu/
https://www.bohcinc.com/
https://www.espeakers.com/marketplace/profile/
44161/Dr-Nefertiti-Fisher

Dr. Nefertiti is a John Maxwell Team certified speaker, teacher, trainer, and coach. She is passionate about personal development in all its forms, but her specialties are teaching and training. Dr. Nefertiti is also an Amazon Best Selling Author with three books on her shelf with more to come. As a certified teacher and trainer with the John Maxwell Team, not only is she equipped with a host of top-tier development resources to share with you but she has also been taught and trained by one of the world's foremost leadership experts, Dr. John C. Maxwell. John Maxwell has been an authority on leadership for more than 40 years, and if he's taught me anything, it's that teaching is ultimately serving. She is here to provide you with the tools you use to multiply your results; She is here to help you grow yourself, your team, and your organization beyond your barriers... and that is why I love what I do.

# The Power of Me - Self Care

By Dr. Nefertiti S Fisher

In the hustle and bustle of modern life, the concept of self-care has emerged as a beacon of hope for individuals seeking to navigate the complexities of personal and professional demands. Self-care is not a luxury; it is a necessity that empowers individuals to maintain their physical, mental, and emotional health. This essay explores the multifaceted nature of self-care, its benefits, and how it can be integrated into daily life to foster resilience and well-being.

Self-care is the practice of taking action to preserve or improve one's own health. It is a conscious choice to prioritize one's own needs and to engage in activities that promote physical, mental, and emotional health. The power of self-care lies in its ability to transform lives by enhancing personal resilience, improving relationships, and contributing to overall happiness and fulfillment.

One of the primary benefits of self-care is the enhancement of physical health. Engaging in regular exercise, eating a balanced diet, getting adequate sleep, and avoiding harmful substances are all forms of self-care that contribute to physical well-being. These practices can reduce the risk of chronic diseases, improve energy levels, and boost the immune system. By taking care of the body, individuals are better equipped to handle the demands of daily life and to recover from illness or injury.

Mental health is another critical area where self-care plays a pivotal role. Stress, anxiety, and depression are common mental health challenges that can be mitigated through self-care practices such as mindfulness, meditation, and engaging in hobbies or activities that bring joy. These practices help to reduce stress levels, improve mood, and enhance cognitive function. By nurturing mental health, individuals can maintain a positive outlook, make better decisions, and build stronger relationships.

Emotional health is equally important, and self-care can help individuals manage and express their emotions in healthy ways. This might involve seeking support from friends or professionals, journaling, or engaging in creative activities that allow for emotional expression. By taking care of their emotional well-being, individuals can develop greater self-awareness, empathy, and resilience in the face of life's challenges.

Self-care is also a powerful tool for fostering resilience. Resilience is the ability to bounce back from adversity, and self-care practices can strengthen an individual's capacity to cope with stress and overcome challenges. By engaging in self-care, individuals build a foundation of strength and well-being that can support them through difficult times. This might include setting boundaries, practicing self-compassion, and engaging in activities that promote relaxation and rejuvenation.

Moreover, **self-care is not a selfish act**; it is an essential component of healthy relationships. When individuals take care of themselves, they are better able to show up for others. They can offer support, empathy, and love without depleting their own resources. Self-care enables individuals to maintain healthy boundaries, communicate effectively, and contribute positively to their relationships.

Integrating self-care into daily life requires intentionality and commitment. It begins with self-awareness—understanding one's own needs and recognizing when self-care is needed. This might involve reflecting on daily routines, identifying stressors, and assessing areas where self-care can be improved.

Setting realistic goals and creating a self-care plan are essential steps. This plan should include a variety of self-care activities tailored to the individual's needs and preferences. It might involve scheduling regular exercise, setting aside time for hobbies, or planning regular check-ins with a therapist or counselor.

Consistency is key in the practice of self-care. Small, daily acts of self-care can have a cumulative effect over time. It is important to approach self-care with flexibility, adjusting practices as needs change and being patient with oneself when progress is slow. That is most important to be patient with oneself, because we put unnecessary pressure on ourselves to be perfect inside of imperfect situations.

Improving mental health through self-care involves a variety of practices that can help manage stress, reduce symptoms of anxiety and depression, and promote overall emotional well-being. Here are some examples of self-care practices specifically aimed at enhancing mental health:

1. **Mindfulness and Meditation**: Engaging in mindfulness exercises or meditation can help calm the mind, reduce stress, and improve focus. Even a few minutes a day can make a significant difference.

2. **Journaling**: Writing down thoughts and feelings in a journal can be a therapeutic way to process emotions, reflect on experiences, and track personal growth.

3. **Physical Exercise**: Regular physical activity, such as walking, jogging, yoga, or dancing, can boost mood and reduce symptoms of anxiety and depression by releasing endorphins.

4. **Adequate Sleep**: Ensuring you get enough sleep is crucial for mental health. Establishing a regular sleep schedule and creating a restful environment can improve sleep quality.

5. **Healthy Eating**: A balanced diet rich in fruits, vegetables, whole grains, and lean proteins can support brain health and mood stability.

6. **Social Connections**: Spending time with friends and loved ones, or even engaging in community activities, can provide emotional support and reduce feelings of isolation.

7. **Professional Support**: Seeking help from mental health professionals, such as therapists or counselors, can provide guidance and support in managing mental health challenges.

8. **Creative Expression**: Engaging in creative activities like painting, drawing, writing, or playing music can be a cathartic way to express emotions and reduce stress.

9. **Digital Detox**: Taking regular breaks from social media and digital devices can reduce exposure to negative news and comparisons, which can impact mental health.

10. **Relaxation Techniques**: Practices such as deep breathing exercises, progressive muscle relaxation, or guided imagery can help manage anxiety and promote relaxation.

11. **Nature and Fresh Air**: Spending time outdoors, whether it's a walk in the park, a hike, or gardening, can improve mood and reduce stress.

12. **Setting Boundaries**: Learning to say no and setting healthy boundaries can prevent burnout and protect your mental health.

13. **Hobbies and Interests**: Dedicating time to hobbies and activities you enjoy can provide a sense of accomplishment and joy.

14. **Gratitude Practice**: Focusing on the things you are grateful for can shift your mindset towards positivity and reduce feelings of depression.

15. **Mindful Breaks**: Taking short breaks throughout the day to practice deep breathing or stretching can help manage stress and improve focus.

Incorporating these self-care practices into your daily routine can help improve mental health and resilience. It's important to find what works best for you and to be consistent in your self-care efforts. Remember, self-care is a personal journey, and what works for one person may not work for another. The key is to be patient with yourself and to make self-care a priority.

In conclusion, the power of self-care is transformative. It is a pathway to well-being and resilience that enables individuals to thrive in all aspects of life. By prioritizing self-care, individuals can enhance their physical, mental, and emotional health, foster resilience, and build stronger relationships. The journey of self-care is a personal one, and it requires intentionality, commitment, and self-awareness. Yet, the rewards are immeasurable, offering a life enriched by health, happiness, and fulfillment. In a world that often demands so much, self-care is the gift we give to ourselves—a reminder that our well-being is worth the effort.

## Felisha Jones

Heal My People
Chief Visionary Officer, Certified Meditation Teacher &
Self-care Activist

https://www.linkedin.com/in/felishajones/
https://www.instagram.com/healingmypeople
https://www.healmypeople.com/

Felisha Jones is a self-care activist who passionately advocates that self-care is preventative care—a scientifically proven and proactive approach that equips people to face life's challenges with ease and clarity. She skillfully weaves affirmations, joy, prayer, and meditation into her sessions; empowering individuals to embrace a restful awareness. Through these practices, she demonstrates how our breath can serve as our medicine to regulate our nervous systems in an increasingly chaotic world.

# Are You Ghosting Yourself? 10 Ways to Snatch Back Your Joy

By Felisha Jones

Have you ever had someone unexpectedly stop talking to you without an explanation? Have you ever wondered why you didn't get the job? Have you ever wanted closure from a partner who ended things abruptly? Is it still haunting you why you weren't invited to speak at the conference?

These situations are examples of being ghosted. It is essentially the practice of ending a relationship with someone by suddenly and without explanation withdrawing from all communication.

Sadly, many of us are ghosting ourselves without realizing it. We are walking around like zombies and robots. We are alive but not living. We have not established our true purpose. We're living someone else's dream. Some of us are following the same exact script on a daily basis without any room for imagination or creativity.

Does this sound like you?

If so, you have essentially ghosted yourself. At some point you have broken communication with yourself and the Spirit within. You have abandoned your dreams and aspirations. You have mentally and spiritually tapped out. You need to put an APB out on your smile—the one that shows all of your teeth. You're probably looking in the mirror each morning wondering who has infiltrated your body.

No worries. I'm not judging. You can reverse this cycle. But, first a reminder...

*She promises herself adventure, new places, different views, a chance to get lost.*

*She infuses her day with newness and wonder.*

*She brings a camera everywhere, notices the little things, gets a cup of coffee at a different cafe, and takes the long way home.*

*She discovers so much unexpected joy. She begins to LOVE the journey.*

~ I Am Her, M.H. Clark

It's time to actively show up for yourself in every way—mentally, emotionally, spiritually, and physically. It's time to establish a mind-body-spirit connection that can't be shaken by the wayward world we're living in right now. It's time to put on your armor and defeat the negativity with positivity. It's time to live knowing that what's meant for you can't miss you. It's time to rise up in your purpose with a relentless pursuit of joy. It's time to live in the present, one deep breath at a time.

## Here are 10 ways to stop ghosting yourself:

1. **Acknowledge Your Feelings**

   Stop ignoring your emotions. Allow your feelings to pass through your body like running water. Yell. Cry. Vent. Punch the bag. Journal, meditate, or pray about what you're feeling instead of suppressing it. Schedule the therapist. Dust off your Bible. Sign up for the yoga class.

2. **Confront Hard Truths**

   Be real (but loving) with yourself. You are your best friend. Write a pros and cons list about your current situation. If something isn't working, acknowledge it, don't avoid it. Make the change.

3. **Practice Self-Compassion**

   Practice the Ho'oponopono Meditation each morning: Close your eyes. Place your hand over your heart. Take a deep breath. Repeat the following to yourself 21 times:

- **I LOVE YOU - I'M SORRY - PLEASE FORGIVE ME - THANK YOU!**
- **I LOVE YOU - I'M SORRY - PLEASE FORGIVE ME - THANK YOU!**
- **I LOVE YOU - I'M SORRY - PLEASE FORGIVE ME - THANK YOU!**

4. **Take Responsibility for Your Life**

Go to a beautiful cafe and pull out your computer. Create. Apply. Make the ask. Knock on the door. No more excuses.

5. **Prioritize Self-Care**

Take a nap. Book the trip. Spend the money. Turn off the TV at 10 p.m. Limit the news and drama. Eat nourishing foods. Dance for 20 minutes. Place flowers in your bath water.

6. **Take Action, Even if It's Small**

Focus on ONE thing each day. Procrastination and perfectionism come from fear. Break things into smaller steps and just start— progress matters more than perfection.

7. **Address Imposter Syndrome**

Comparison is the thief of joy and progress. YOU belong anywhere you want to be. Your bloodline is beautiful and they deserve to shine through you.

8. **Set Boundaries**

Say "NO" to things that don't align with your values or well-being. Protect your time and energy from things that don't serve you. Place the oxygen on yourself first and then help others.

9. **Leave Toxic Relationships**

If someone is draining your energy, disrespecting your boundaries, or keeping you stuck, it's time to let them go—respectfully. Prioritize relationships that support your growth. Find your people. Grow with your people. Family should exude love, not jealousy or hate.

## 10. Seek Out a Self-Care Plan

Self-care is a way of life. Each day should begin with YOU in mind. Sometimes, you just need a little help adjusting your lifestyle to accommodate what you desire most. If you're ready to stop ghosting yourself, email me at Hello@HealmyPeople.com. I'm so excited to hear from you.

*I will not die an unlived life. I will not live in fear of falling or catching fire.*

*I choose to inhabit my days, to allow living to open me, to make me less afraid, more accessible; to loosen my heart until it becomes a wing, a torch, a promise.*

*I choose to risk my significance, to live so that which came to me as seed goes to the next as blossom, and that which came to me as blossom, goes on as fruit.*

~ I Am Her, M.H. Clark

## Becca Elan

Owner of BeccaElan
Author/Artist

https://www.facebook.com/beccaelan
https://www.instagram.com/beccaelan/
https://beccaelan.com/

BeccaElan is a celebrated artist and philanthropist. As a mother of two neurodivergent children, she passionately supports their journey through life, leveraging her personal experiences to provide comprehensive resources for others. Her work is dedicated to aiding neurodivergent individuals in managing their emotions and thriving in society. BeccaElan graduated with a JD, focusing on contract law with a minor in psychology, and is certified in mental health and alternative dispute resolution. She combines her legal expertise and mental health knowledge to advocate for comprehensive support systems. BeccaElan also provides daily guidance to her followers with inspiring messages, helping others find strength and inspiration in their daily lives. Her commitment to mental health advocacy and support is reflected in all aspects of her life and work, making her a beacon of hope, guidance, and positivity for many who seek her advice, wisdom, and compassionate support.

# From Shadows to Light: A Journey of Healing and Self-Discovery as a Parent of Neurodivergent Children

By Becca Elan

Hello beautiful Souls! It is with great purpose and heartfelt intention that I share this valuable knowledge with you. My main goal is to support your personal growth as a parent of wonderful neurodivergent children. Parenting is a journey filled with joy, challenges, and profound moments of connection, and navigating the unique experiences of raising any child. And being a parent of a neurodivergent child adds an extra layer of complexity and beauty.

In this chapter, you will find a blend of insights, practical advice, and heartfelt stories designed to empower and guide you. As a mother of two neurodivergent children, I understand the unique challenges and triumphs that come with this journey. My experiences have taught me invaluable lessons, which I am eager to share with you.

It can be easy to get caught up in the daily struggles and challenges that come with caring for my unique and wonderful kids. However, I have learned that in order to be the best caregiver for my children, I must also take care of myself. Recognizing and acknowledging my own needs is the first step towards achieving a healthy and balanced life as a parent.

Remember, it's perfectly okay to have your own dreams and needs outside of being a parent! It's not selfish to focus on your happiness and well-being. Actually, when you take care of yourself, you're even better at taking care of your children. You can't pour from an empty cup, so make sure you're topped up and ready to rock!

Being a parent to a neurodivergent child can sometimes feel like a rollercoaster of emotions. It's easy to slip into feelings of guilt and self-blame, especially when your child has aggressive reactions. It's important to remember that these outbursts aren't intentional—it's just their overwhelmed brain struggling to cope. I've been there, questioning every decision and wondering if I'm doing enough. But those feelings don't define you as a parent! When I realized this, I started focusing on understanding and supporting my child's unique needs. For example, instead of blaming myself for my child's meltdowns, I learned to recognize the triggers and create a calming environment. It made a world of difference!

Let's be real, parenting can sometimes feel like a wild ride on a rollercoaster! There were times when I felt like my emotions were taking control, leaving me feeling like I was making monstrous waves without even realizing it. I knew I had to hit the pause button and check in with myself to be fully present for my children. It dawned on me that to be the amazing mom I wanted to be, I had to heal myself first. And no, I'm not just talking about a spa day or a mini adult vacay—I'm talking about diving deep into who you are and why you react the way you do. It's like trying to drive a car with an empty tank—you've got to refuel yourself to keep going strong!

One of the most transformative tools I have discovered in my quest for balance and well-being is the ancient art of energy healing or Shadow Work. Before I discovered a more harmonious flow on this journey, I was like a circus performer trying to juggle flaming torches while riding a unicycle—except the torches were my past issues, and the unicycle was my sanity. Those pesky unresolved problems kept sneaking up on me, which my children and I called the "Ferves," causing me to react to my kids in ways that were less than healthy. This led to a whirlwind of deep depression, overwhelming stress, and a body that felt like it was constantly waving a white flag of surrender. I was perpetually sick and knew things had to change!

When my late friend Pearry Teo[3] reached out and invited me to be a copyeditor for his book on Shadow Work, it felt like I had just discovered a secret treasure map for my mind. Picture me, already drowning in the chaotic sea of parenting, stumbling through emotional storms, and feeling lost. Pearry's invitation seemed like a magical key that could unlock a new world of understanding. I remember thinking, "Seriously?! Are you telling me I get to dive into this mysterious world of Shadow Work and experience it myself? This sounds incredible!"

Of course, I wasn't just handed the map and told to sail away. No way. Shadow Work turned out to be more like a deep dive into an ancient, mystical cave—one filled with twists, turns, and hidden surprises. At first, it felt like I was opening Pandora's box. I plunged into a session, and let me tell you, it was like I had unleashed a wild rollercoaster of emotions. There I was, confronting a fear of inadequacy that had been lurking in my shadows like a dormant dragon. It was like unearthing a monster I had buried under layers of my past. I vividly recalled sneaking down the stairs as a child, overhearing my parents discussing a teacher's negative comment about me. My little kid brain twisted their concern into a belief that I wasn't good enough. That shadow of misunderstanding had loomed over me, making me a more controlling and overbearing parent than I ever intended to be.

Here's where it gets intense: As I faced this fear head-on, tears streamed down my face. It felt like a storm raging inside me, but then—suddenly—a warm, flickering light of self-compassion began to glow. This light was like a lighthouse guiding me through the emotional storm. With each breath, it grew brighter, lifting a heavy cloak from my shoulders. For the first time in years, I felt revitalized, as if I had discovered a new source of energy and was finally ready to face whatever came my way!

---

[3] *Shadow Work: Finding Your Light in Darkness (THE COMPLETE SHADOW WORK COLLECTION by DR. AIWASS UKEHI)*

But the adventure didn't stop there. As I worked through my shadows, I began to see the ripples of change in my family. Take my daughter with Asperger's, for example. She had always struggled with noisy environments, and I had missed a crucial clue. When I finally noticed her need for noise-canceling headphones, it was like finding the missing piece of a puzzle. Family gatherings transformed into enjoyable experiences for her, where she could be part of the fun without feeling overwhelmed. It was like watching her step into a magical world where she could truly thrive.

Then came the cliffhanger moment with my oldest daughter. She was a brilliant, curious mind, but self-doubt often clouded her path. Inspired by my own journey, I introduced her to mindfulness and affirmations. Our new routine became a heartwarming adventure, turning every challenge into a chance for growth. One day, she faced a particularly tricky task and was on the verge of giving up. I held my breath, hoping her new techniques would work. She applied these, the ones she developed for herself, and guess what? She succeeded, it was like witnessing a phoenix rise from the ashes. Her confidence soared, and I felt an overwhelming rush of pride and relief.

One rainy afternoon, I saw her retreat to her tent, looking like she was about to burst into tears. My heart raced—was my idea a total flop? It dawned on me that this little retreat was more than just a tent; it was her space to regroup and recover from the overwhelming "Ferves" of her day. Then, something amazing happened. When she emerged later, her face lit up with a beaming smile, and she looked as relaxed as a cat lounging in a sunbeam. It was like we had created a secret garden where she could recharge and find her own peace. Seeing her so content was a victory that filled our home with warmth and a deeper understanding of each other's needs. As she grew, the tent transformed into a cozy haven, with each room serving as a sanctuary. Eventually, she found ways to find peace and solace in any situation. However, she still retreats to her safe haven room for some much-needed decompression. Don't we all crave a space like that!

The plot thickened with our family dynamics in ways I hadn't anticipated. Picture this: I found myself in the middle of a heated argument with my youngest daughter, and tensions were running high. Drawing on my newfound empathy and communication skills from Shadow Work, I took a deep breath and employed breathing techniques to steady my nerves. I also reminded myself to ask for guidance on what needed to be said and what was best left unsaid—a technique I had learned to help me navigate the turbulence.

It felt like I was wielding a superpower as I addressed her feelings with kindness rather than frustration. I told my anxious inner child that it was okay to express my emotions calmly and to speak with kindness, not meanness. My calm and understanding approach, paired with these techniques, helped us work through the conflict more smoothly than I ever imagined. It was like watching a turbulent sea calm into a serene lake. Thank you, Pearry! Shadow Work was just the magic we needed to turn our family challenges into opportunities for connection and growth.

As I journeyed through Shadow Work, the impact on my personal well-being was nothing short of transformative. What once felt like a never-ending struggle with depression and anxiety began to shift dramatically. Though these challenges are still a work in progress, they're now 100 times better than before.

For instance, I remember days when anxiety would seize me like an uninvited guest. But Shadow Work gave me the tools to address these feelings with compassion rather than frustration. Breathing techniques and gentle self-talk became my allies, helping me to calm my anxious child self and navigate tough moments with a newfound sense of calm.

Even my physical health began to flourish. I recall how Shadow Work helped me shed the heavy cloak of stress and fatigue that had been dragging me down. Suddenly, I felt more energized and alive, like I'd been given a new lease on life. My health improvements were like the cherry on top of this healing journey, making me feel more vibrant and ready to embrace each day.

So, our home became more than just a place of growth—it turned into a haven where every challenge was met with resilience, every lesson was a step toward healing, and every day was a new opportunity to celebrate love and well-being. Thanks to Shadow Work, the journey has not only healed my mind and body but also enriched our family's lives in ways I never imagined.

So, here I am, at the end of this chapter, feeling like a seasoned adventurer who's navigated through storms and emerged with a clearer mind and a lighter heart. My children and I are thriving, and the journey of self-discovery has been both challenging and profoundly rewarding. The healing continues, and every day feels like a new page in our story of transformation and joy.

## Debra Soul

Healing by Soul
Creator

https://www.facebook.com/Dgoodsoul/
https://www.instagram.com/healing_by_soul
https://www.healingbysoul.com/

Master Integrated Energy Therapist aka Healing with the Angels Chakra to Aura Balancing Certified Medium Past Regression & Future Life Specialist Ghost whisperer Aromatherapist Author of "Healing by Soul - A Journey to Joy" & "The Sound of Your Soul Workbook" Unity Reverend Debra Soul is a channel for angels, guides and ancestors to heal clients worldwide. Her sessions, tailored to individual needs, transcend traditional psychiatric methods, facilitating soul-to-soul healings, for the highest good and karmic lesson resolutions. Notable achievements include healing from the core of the issues from every energy field, physical, mental, emotional & karmic/past life issues, transitioning unwanted entities, miraculous healings, and supporting special needs clients. Debra studied with prominent teachers such as Steven Thayer, Reverend Stephen Robinson, and Dr. Josh Axe. Her profound connection to the spiritual realm and extensive expertise of 20 years, makes her a beacon for holistic healings; bringing clarity, peace, and transformation to her clients.

# From Darkness to Light: My Journey to Empowerment

By Debra Soul

My life was a whirlwind of chaos, but you would never know it by looking at me. I wore a mask of normalcy, hiding the turmoil within.

Living with my ex-husband was like walking on eggshells. The fear was constant. The unpredictability of his moods kept me on edge. At times, he could be charming but those moments were fleeting. Mostly, he was cruel and controlling. He would lock me in the bathroom or confine me to my room on many occasions, making me feel like I was the cause, deserving this cruel treatment. He was a narcissist, but I could not see it through my turmoil. The emotional scars he left on my heart were deep, painful and eventually got me physically ill.

The stress and fear took a toll on my health. I developed an arrhythmia that Doctors and Specialists were baffled by and could not cure. My heart rate plummeted to dangerously low levels in the low 20 range. I was constantly dizzy. I was distraught and miserable. I could not care for my two young children nor work as a caseworker for special needs children.

A friend suggested I see a holistic healer. Desperate for relief, I made an appointment. During the session, she never touched me. All she did was flip through the pages of a book. I felt a strange sensation in my belly, and when the session was over, I was able to stand and walk with newfound energy. I was back!

I asked "what this was? she replied, "Consegrity -Healing with Vibrational Words".

This experience was life-changing. No doctor could cure me, but vibrational words did. I did not understand it, but I was so ecstatic. I knew I had to learn this mysterious technique.

I took the course and it gave me a curiosity to delve further into other holistic practices. The modality that resonated with me the most was Integrated Energy Therapy, aka, Healing with the Angels. This angel healing energy technique transformed my life, both physically and emotionally.

I was trapped in a mentally abusive marriage, and the angels guided me. They have been with me throughout this new journey. They taught me about my mission, guiding me to heal and teach others about angel healing. They revealed the depths of my soul to me.

I realized fear had kept me paralyzed in a toxic relationship for far too long. It wasn't easy to confront it. I had to learn how to overcome the fear within me. That was a significant part of my journey;part of my karmic lesson to be learned. I realized that fear is magnifying the unknown. To overcome it, I had to take small, deliberate steps towards reclaiming my power.

First, I acknowledged my fear. I stopped pretending that everything was fine and faced the reality of my situation. This honesty was painful but necessary. I began to understand that fear thrives in silence and secrecy. By speaking out and seeking support from friends and professionals, the fear began to weaken.

I educated myself- Knowledge is a powerful antidote to fear. I read books, attended workshops, and learned about narcissistic abuse and its effects. Understanding the dynamics of my relationship helped me see that the problem wasn't me; it was the toxic environment I was in. This realization was liberating and gave me the strength to take action.

I practiced self-compassion. I had been so hard on myself, blaming myself for staying in the relationship for so long. But I learned to forgive myself and recognize that I did the best I could with the knowledge and resources I had at the time. This self-compassion allowed me to heal and move forward without the burden of guilt.

Building a support network was crucial. I reached out to friends, family, and support groups. Their encouragement and understanding provided a safety net that caught me when I felt like I was falling. They reminded me that I wasn't alone and that there was a community of people who cared about my well-being.

Finally, I took action. It was baby steps at first, like setting boundaries and asserting my needs. Each step, no matter how small, was a victory. I began to see that I had the power to change my circumstances. The more I acted, the more my confidence grew, and the fear began to dissipate.

Fear to me became:

F- false
E- emotions
A- appearing
R- real

My angels guided me from the very beginning of my awareness and continue to do so daily. I was taught to call upon my angels every morning with gratitude and a specific intention. This practice has become my morning prayers and meditation intertwined. I learned that no one is ever truly stuck in a situation; change is always possible, no matter how daunting it may seem. It starts with a single step, a decision to no longer accept the status quo.

By believing in your own strength and seeking support, you can overcome any obstacle. You can call upon your angels or whatever your belief is. Turn to friends, religion, or energy healing—whatever resonates within you.

Remember, you have the power to rewrite your story and create a life filled with joy and fulfillment. If it was possible for me, it is possible for you.

Nothing is impossible—just think, "I'm possible!"

Today, I am the author of "Healing by Soul: A Journey to Joy" and "The Sound of the Soul Workbook." I have a thriving Holistic Energy Healing Practice. soul-level healing.

No matter how dark it seems, there is always a way to find your light to shine brightly. I am grateful for my healing journey and would love to help you with yours.

Debra Soul
www.healingbysoul.com

Master Angel Energy Healer / Teacher
Certified Medium
Past Life Regression - Future Life Readings
Wedding Officiant

## Jennifer Ritt

Owner of The Ritt Path, LLC

https://www.linkedin.com/in/therittpath/
https://www.facebook.com/jenn.ritt.9/
https://www.instagram.com/jennritthypnohealth/
https://therittpath.com/

I help sensitive, heart-led entrepreneurs break free from overwhelm, burnout, and business strategies that don't align with their energy. Using my 4-part signature system of subconscious reprogramming with Advanced Conversational Hypnosis, emotional intelligence training, nervous system regulation, and holistic health, I guide my clients to build businesses that feel good and create lasting success. Many sensitive entrepreneurs struggle with self-doubt, overwhelm, analysis paralysis and forcing themselves into strategies that drain them. The problem isn't them, it's that they've been trying to build success in a way that doesn't match who they are. I show them a new way: one where business flows effortlessly, success comes from embodiment and alignment (not hustle), and self-trust becomes the foundation of their business. When they shift their energy, their business transforms.

# Ignite Your Shine with Unapologetic Self-Love

By Jennifer Ritt

I believe each woman carries a unique blueprint to health and healing that is deeply shaped by her experiences, the lessons learned from those around her, and the conditioning she's absorbed throughout her life.

When I was a kid, I won a Young Authors award for a story I wrote. I remember how excited I was—I could barely contain it. I felt so proud that I had done something truly special. But that excitement didn't last long.

"Knock it off. It's not polite to brag," my parents said. And just like that, my joy was shut down. "You'll make your sister feel bad."

In that moment, I learned that pride and accomplishment weren't things to be celebrated; they were things to feel guilty about. So instead, I felt shame and learned it was more acceptable to play in the shadows than to shine my light.

I was taught to play small, put others first, and downplay my talents and abilities. So, I spent a lifetime molding myself into what I thought others wanted.

This led me down a path of settling for abusive relationships and jobs that left me feeling exhausted and empty.

I'll never forget one of the first sessions I had with a life coach as I explained how I was living my life. He said, "How does it feel to be living a lie?"

It hit me like a ton of bricks. I realized I had sold myself out. I had buried my voice, my passions, and my talents so deep, that I didn't even know myself anymore.

How many of you have spent your life trying to be everything to everyone, even if it meant sacrificing your own happiness?

I believe our God-given gifts were given to us for a reason. We are here to live our purpose and share our genius in a way that only we can.

But to do that, we have to honor our gifts and our purpose. We must put ourselves first because when we nurture our well-being and let our cups overflow, we can show up for others in a more powerful, authentic way.

That session was my wake-up call to step into my true purpose of helping others. I've always been fascinated with the body's natural ability to heal itself when given the right tools. It was a passion I had explored for years, soaking up as much knowledge as I could find. Suddenly, it all clicked. I went back to school and earned my certification in Holistic Nutrition. I learned how our habits and the foods we eat are powerful medicines to help heal and support our bodies in ways I never fully understood before.

But I still had to deal with those pesky limiting beliefs that doubted and made me fear going after my dreams. But soon, I discovered that once you take that first step into your purpose, the right opportunities and mentors appear to support your journey.

One day, while watching a webinar on natural healing, an advertisement popped up for something called Rapid Transformation Therapy. I was hooked. Using the power of hypnosis to heal trauma and rewire old conditioning and beliefs was the missing piece I had been looking for. I knew that combining the healing power of nutrition with hypnosis to help people break through years of conditioning was something that would help me transform women's lives.

Looking back now, every step of my journey makes sense.

Is there a dream or goal you've buried or abandoned because it felt too big or scary?

As a lifelong people-pleaser with big emotions, one of the hardest and most important things I had to learn was how to set boundaries. I realized I was constantly saying yes to things that didn't fulfill me, just to avoid feeling lonely. I was prioritizing people who I thought cared about me but weren't there for me when it really mattered. So, I made the decision to start honoring myself and stopped saying yes out of guilt or need, and things started to shift. At times I felt very alone, as old relationships that no longer fit fell away. But gradually, as I began to say yes to people who valued me, to experiences that fulfilled my soul, and to choices that put me closer to my goals, my life began to transform.

What I have found is that when you step into your purpose and start putting yourself first, you begin to remember those things that used to light you up.

I pulled the fancy camera I hadn't touched in years out of the closet and started snapping beautiful sunsets, vibrant flowers in bloom, birds, and dragonflies in flight.

I began setting aside time before bed to indulge in a soothing bedtime ritual: a hot bath infused with lavender and rose oils, a steaming cup of hot herbal tea, and a fiction page-turner that's so good it's impossible to put down.

I felt emotions again, ones that had been buried so long ago, really feeling them, but out of self-love this time and not judgment.

I started listening to music again and, to my surprise, discovered a passion for opera I never knew I had.

Cooking a meal became a nurturing act of self-care, not just a necessity. I pick out a nourishing recipe, make a special trip to the farmers' market to gather fresh ingredients, and prepare it, savoring each step.

What is one thing you love to do that you've forsaken?

Life isn't about giving until we are empty; it's about filling our souls with what lights us up so we can give from a place of joy and love.

Stepping into my purpose, rediscovering my passions, and deciding what no longer fits has been a process and a journey of unapologetic self-love. I have had to unlearn, heal, and expand in ways I could never have imagined.

I never expected to take this approach in a book about self-care, but my journey has been anything but traditional. For me, self-care isn't just about rituals and routines. It's about realizing that shining your light is necessary. Honoring yourself is not selfish, nor does it diminish anyone else's light. Imagine what the world would look like if we all allowed ourselves to shine as brightly as possible.

## Dania Trapani

Nutritional Therapist & Health Coach

https://www.facebook.com/profile.php?id=100065627226669
https://www.instagram.com/daniatrapani

I am a nutritional therapist and health coach with 17 years of experience, dedicated to helping women over 40 regain confidence, improve gut health, and build a healthy, sustainable relationship with food. My approach is rooted in nutrition, mindset, and habit transformation, empowering women to feel vibrant, strong, and in control of their well-being.

I believe in nourishing the body, not restricting it, and guiding women toward long-term health without dieting or deprivation. Through my work, I support clients in overcoming emotional eating, improving digestion, and adopting habits that enhance their energy, metabolism, and overall quality of life.

Using a blend of science-backed nutrition, practical strategies, and compassionate coaching, I help my clients break free from unhealthy cycles and step into a lifestyle of balance, joy, and self-trust.

# From Emotional Eating to Empowered Eating: Rebuilding Your Relationship with Food

By Dania Trapani

## Introduction: The Emotional Eating Trap

It starts as a whisper—an urge to reach for something comforting after a long day. Maybe it's a handful of chocolate, a glass of wine, or a plate of something rich and indulgent. Before you know it, the whisper becomes a habit, and food becomes more than just nourishment—it turns into a source of comfort, a distraction, a way to fill the void.

For many women, especially those over 40, emotional eating isn't just about cravings. It's about stress, exhaustion, and years of putting others first. It's about the nights spent unwinding with food because self-care felt like an afterthought. It's about the deep, often unspoken emotions—loneliness, anxiety, frustration, even boredom—that food temporarily soothes.

But here's the truth: Food was never meant to heal emotions. It was never meant to replace self-love, rest, or the deeper needs we often ignore. Emotional eating isn't a sign of failure—it's a signal. A message from within telling us that something deeper needs attention.

The good news? You don't have to stay stuck in this cycle. You can shift from emotional eating to empowered eating, where food becomes a source of nourishment, not a coping mechanism. And when you do, something incredible happens—you reclaim your power, your body, and your sense of self.

## The Science of Emotional Eating: Why We Crave What We Crave

Emotional eating is not about willpower. It's about biology, psychology, and habit loops that have been reinforced over time.

When we're stressed, anxious, or overwhelmed, our body releases cortisol, the stress hormone that increases cravings for high-fat, high-sugar foods. Why? Because those foods provide a temporary dopamine hit—a surge of pleasure and relief. This is why we don't crave carrots when we're stressed; we crave cookies, chips, and comfort foods that give us a quick emotional escape.

But that relief is fleeting. The real issue remains untouched, and we find ourselves stuck in a pattern: Stress → Craving → Eating → Guilt → More Stress.

And for women over 40, this pattern can feel even harder to break. Hormonal fluctuations—declining oestrogen, insulin resistance, and changes in serotonin—can increase cravings and emotional sensitivity. Add in years of dieting, food guilt, and body image struggles, and it's no wonder emotional eating becomes a deeply ingrained response.

But here's the thing: Once you understand the cycle, you can change it.

## Self-Awareness: Identifying Emotional Hunger vs. Physical Hunger

Before reaching for food, pause and ask yourself:

> *Am I truly hungry, or am I looking for comfort?*
> *What am I feeling right now? Stressed? Lonely? Overwhelmed?*
> *Is there something else I need besides food?*

This simple act of awareness creates space between impulse and action. It allows you to make a conscious choice rather than an automatic reaction.

If you're truly hungry, eat. But if it's emotional hunger, consider what else might nourish you.

## Mindful Eating: Savouring, Not Stuffing

Mindful eating isn't just about slowing down—it's about being present with food.

Eat without distractions. Turn off the TV, put down your phone, and allow yourself to experience your meal.

Savour each bite. Notice the flavours, textures, and how the food makes you feel.

Pause halfway through. Ask yourself, *Am I still hungry, or am I eating out of habit?*

When you eat with awareness, you naturally regain control. Food no longer controls you—you control how you engage with it.

## Healthy Coping Mechanisms: Replacing Food with Self-Care

If food has become your go-to comfort, it's time to expand your toolbox. Instead of using food to soothe emotions, try:

- Movement. A short walk, stretching, or dancing in your kitchen can shift your emotional state.
- Breathing exercises. Deep, intentional breathing lowers cortisol and calms the mind.
- Journalling. Writing out your feelings helps process emotions rather than suppress them.
- Connection. Calling a friend, hugging a loved one, or simply being in nature can provide the emotional nourishment you truly need.

Food is one way to comfort yourself—but it's not the only way. When you give yourself other forms of care, food loses its power as an emotional crutch.

## Food as Nourishment, Not Punishment

For many women, food has been tied to guilt, restriction, and cycles of control for decades. But it doesn't have to be this way. What if food was simply nourishment? What if it was fuel for your body, instead of a battleground?

Shifting the mindset from restriction to empowerment changes everything. Instead of focusing on what you "shouldn't eat," focus on what your body needs to thrive.

Eat for energy, not emotion. Choose foods that fuel you, not drain you.

Enjoy indulgences without guilt. A piece of cake doesn't ruin your progress—your mindset around it does.

Honour your hunger. Eating when you're hungry and stopping when you're satisfied is an act of self-trust.

Food is not your enemy. It is your ally in feeling strong, vibrant, and alive.

## Your Glow-Up Plan: A New Way Forward

Breaking free from emotional eating isn't about perfection—it's about progress. It's about choosing, day by day, to tune in to what your body and soul truly need.

Start small. Choose one mindful eating practice to implement this week.

Create a self-care ritual. The next time you feel an emotional craving, try a non-food comfort strategy first.

Forgive yourself. Emotional eating is part of being human. When it happens, approach yourself with kindness, not judgement.

Listen to your body. It is always speaking—your job is to slow down and listen.

## Final Thoughts: Reclaiming Your Power

You are not weak for struggling with emotional eating. You are not undisciplined or broken. You are a woman who has spent years caring for others, navigating stress, and doing the best you could with what you knew.

But now? You know more. And with that knowledge comes power— the power to heal, to change, and to build a new relationship with food, one based on self-trust, nourishment, and joy.

This journey isn't about deprivation or dieting. It's about coming home to yourself. It's about learning that you are worthy of care—not just through food, but through the way you speak to yourself, the way you honour your needs, and the way you choose to glow from the inside out.

Because when you stop using food to silence your emotions and start using self-care to nurture yourself, you don't just eat differently—you live differently.

And that is where the real glow begins.

## Serena Laursen

Life Coach & Yoga Teacher

https://www.linkedin.com/in/serena-laursen/
https://www.facebook.com/serenalaursen
https://serenalaursen.com/

Serena Laursen is a wife, mom, grandma, Life Coach and Yoga Teacher. She is rooted in empathy, trust, and a deep understanding of one's soul desires and potential. She worked at Microsoft for 20 years, earning six figures while supporting hundreds of team members and leaders, and secretly struggled part of her career with stress and pain. Today, when she's not going on nature walks, practicing yoga, connecting with friends, and spending quality time with family, you'll often find her helping professionals who are overwhelmed, exhausted, and always "doing" at the expense of their health and inner peace. Helping them to slow down, connect with their body to release stress and tension, and cultivate a home and work life that feels grounded and expansive. To learn more about Serena Laursen and how she can help you find your version of wellness that resonates and feels natural to you, visit serenalaursen.com.

# Healing and Growing from the Corporate World Through Coaching and Yoga

By Serena Laursen

"Life-changing!" That's the word that comes to mind, when I think about how incorporating wellness and self-care into my life has been personally and professionally a nurturing and healing experience.

I worked in the corporate world for 20 years, earning a six-figure salary while supporting hundreds of team members and leaders. During this period in my life, I wasn't taking the best care of myself. I wasn't connected with my being or expressing myself fully from my mind, body, and heart. I was constantly DOING, DOING, DOING... always trying to meet others' expectations. But how could I know what others expected? I didn't ask; I just assumed.

During this time, I ventured out, starting my life coaching business, driven by my belief that self-care and life balance are essential for our overall well-being. Through coaching, I learned that these assumptions were just thoughts, unconfirmed by others. I began to listen to my inner wisdom and reflect on my true desires, which allowed me to express myself authentically.

Today, I am a life coach and yoga teacher, combining both practices to help others find balance and well-being in their lives.

## Overcoming Challenges

During my years of constant activity, I lost sight and focus of my life, not realizing what I had achieved. I was working non-stop, always online, and not present with my family. I was neglecting my body by drinking too much soda and not being thoughtful about what I ate. I ignored my body's needs and suppressed stress, leading to various aches and pains. I remember struggling to cut and prep dinner due to pain in my hands and wrists.

A heavy experience was when our home was burglarized. That same year, I ended up in the emergency room on the night of a friend's "Celebration of Life" service. These were my signs from the Universe that something needed to change, and I realized that I was striving towards everything I already had and wanted... a beautiful home and a loving family.

I realized the importance of balancing priorities, wants, needs, and self-care, so I began seeing a naturopath, taking vitamins and supplements, and drinking more water consistently. I was even able to eliminate my soda habit! Spending time with loved ones and doing what I love became non-negotiable. I created boundaries around my time and energy. Developing personal commitment plans and affirmations that resonated with my thoughts, desires, needs, and aspirations supported my new boundaries.

## Practices and Perspectives

I believe self-care and life balance are vital for our well-being. I teach others to become present, feel their feelings, and embrace their own thoughts and beliefs, rather than just doing what they think is expected. Each soul is unique; thus, I help them develop practices that truly resonate personally.

One of the fundamental concepts that I learned from coaching and now share is called "States of Presence." Being completely present allows someone to be in one place at a time, vulnerable and authentic. We can be more in the now when we are in four states of presence: physical, mental, emotional, and spiritual. During my life coach training, I often cried (becoming overwhelmed by emotion) when listening to someone being coached or when I was coached. As a coaching ambassador, I learned to manage my emotional state by engaging with all four states of presence. I physically sat up, looked around the room, mentally acknowledged all students, felt gratitude, and let my emotions float away without suppression. This practice helped me be fully present and connected.

I also teach Yin Yoga as another way to connect in the moment, which involves finding stillness while holding poses. Over time, this practice can bring people into the four States of Presence, clear the mind of external distractions, and support the body's natural healing abilities by releasing tension at deeper levels.

Additionally, I help others set realistic, achievable goals that align with their values, cultivating balance along the way. The power of support, accountability, and personal growth harmonizes with taking intentional steps toward one's desires and dreams.

## Embracing Wellness

Throughout my journey, I have learned that self-care and life balance are not just concepts but essential practices for a fulfilling life. By integrating coaching and yoga, I guide others to find their own unique paths to wellness. Each person's journey is different, and finding what is important and works for them is essential.

Through my experiences, I have resonated with a deep sense of being present, setting boundaries, and prioritizing self-care. These practices have not only changed my life but also empowered me to help others on their wellness journeys. I collaborate with my clients by utilizing a combination of coaching and yoga to connect mind, body, and heart to set realistic, achievable goals that align with their values, develop individualized commitment plans and affirmations, be intentional and in the Four States of Presence, and prioritize balance in their lives. By sharing my story, experiences, and thoughts, I hope to inspire other women to embrace their wellness and self-care, leading to a more balanced and fulfilling life.

## Michele Gunn

Founder of Cultivate and Thrive
Self-Actualization Coach

https://www.linkedin.com/in/michelegunn/
https://www.facebook.com/michele.jonasgunn/
https://www.instagram.com/michelegunn1
https://www.michelegunn.com/

As a Gallup-Certified Strengths Coach and founder of Cultivate and Thrive, Michele Gunn empowers individuals through self-actualization (knowing and embracing self) to embrace their God-given strengths and live purposefully. Since 2018, Michele's faith-based mission has centered on helping people recognize their unique gifts to foster success and fulfillment in all areas of life. Michele's rich experience across family life and various industries brings a wide perspective and deep understanding to her work. A committed Christian, contributing author, and podcast host of Cultivate to Thrive, she guides women in building lives rooted in faith and inner strength to thrive in the fulfilling life they were created for. To learn more about Michele and how she can help you embrace all you were created for, connect with her and Cultivate and Thrive on Facebook, Instagram, LinkedIn, or visit her website at www.michelegunn.com. It's time to put you back in your life!

# Reclaiming Your Strength Through Mental Fitness, Positivity and Gratitude

By Michele Gunn

The world can be a tough place to be! With the rise of social media and the "What's in it for me" mentality, people seldom think about other people in a positive way. School was a tough environment, but now the workplace can be just as bad. As women, we are often taught that every other woman is our competition. We need to make sure that the competition does not win, no matter the cost. Many women are feeling beaten down, unsuccessful or lost, even when outsiders believe their life is perfect. If this describes you, you need wellness and self-care! Incorporating wellness and self-care has given me the mental, emotional and physical strength to pivot on my life journey and live the life God created me to live, personally and professionally.

You may suffer from (as I have and do) negative thoughts that self-destruct. This can be found in what is called Imposter Syndrome, or it can just be there nagging and chipping away at your self-confidence and your self-value. I am overcoming (I will always be a work in progress) this challenge by strengthening my mental fitness, practicing a positive perspective and living in gratitude.

There are no truly unique perspectives or practices. You need to find what works for you. It is in learning who you are, embracing your strengths and aiming them through a positive mindset where you can build that foundation of inner strength to overcome and forge forward!

## Let's Talk About Mental Fitness

Do you have nagging thoughts about how you could have or should have done something better? Do you often wonder if you are good enough or strong enough to accomplish something? Do you think that you do not deserve to be successful? If so, you are not alone.

According to a variety of studies, a large number of people, as much as 70%, report that they feel they are "not good enough." This is particularly present in women. The exact numbers can vary depending on the specific study and people surveyed.

It is time to get a handle on those thoughts. Building your mental fitness will help you be in control of your thoughts, which in turn, control how you perceive and function in life. Start small so you can make progress without feeling like you failed. Here are some tips to implement:

- Practice focusing on an object, letting your mind be free of thoughts.
- Sit with your eyes closed and focus on hearing a specific sound in the environment without thinking about what it is or what is causing it.
- Sit with your eyes closed and focus on your breathing: breathe in, breathe out.

Do these exercises (one or more) several times a day if possible. Start with a small length of time (10 seconds) and build to three minutes. The purpose is to learn to control your thoughts, so when needed, you can change what and how you are thinking.

## Let's Talk About Practicing a Positive Perspective

Are you a "glass half empty" or a "glass half full" person? I have always been a glass-half-empty person and work very hard to be a "glass overflowing" person. A "glass half empty" person sees what can go wrong and how they can lose what they have. That is their focus. A "glass half full" person sees things in a positive way. They see the good of what is, and the potential that can be. A "glass overflowing" person sees things in abundance. There is more available than can be kept. The "glass half empty" perspective is negative. It comes from a scarcity perspective and is driven by fear. The "glass half full" is a positive perspective of what can be. Focus on the "glass overflowing" perspective. This perspective of abundance is rooted in positivity. A positive perspective puts you in a position to be open to opportunity.

Here are some tips to help change your perspective to a positive one:

- Look for gifts and opportunities at each moment.
- Focus on what is right rather than what is wrong.
- Be intentional with positivity. Shake off negative thoughts.

## Let's Talk About Living in Gratitude

"The quality of being thankful; readiness to show appreciation for and to return kindness," is a definition of gratitude from the Oxford Languages Dictionary. To live in gratitude, you must recognize the blessings and opportunities in life. You understand the gifts that other people provide through daily living, whether it be at home, work, friendships or during other activities.

To live in gratitude, practice being grateful. Here are some tips to follow:

- Start each day by journaling or speaking about what you are grateful for.
- During the day, notice good things. Practice thanking people for things they do or things they say.
- At the end of each day, make a list of things you are grateful for.

Keeping gratitude in the front of your mind, will help keep you centered in your positive perspective as well as help you grow your mental fitness.

## What I Was to Who I Am

I used to focus on what was wrong with me, what I couldn't have, what could go wrong and how other people were more successful than me. I have strengthened my mental fitness to keep that negative self-talk out of my head. I embrace my strengths and talents of who I am created to be. I hold a positive perspective to see the good that is and can be, allowing opportunities to be seen. I live in gratitude, recognizing all I have, all I am and all I can give.

Using this type of self-care for total wellness has enabled me to flourish in my life's journey, both personally and professionally. After all, we are a whole person, not just one dimension of what we do or who we are!

Now, it is your turn to live intentionally with mental fitness, positivity and gratitude!

## Neelofer Basaria, DrPH

Founder of True Living
Coach

https://www.linkedin.com/in/neelofer-basaria-drph-23997817/
https://www.facebook.com/neelofer.basaria
https://www.instagram.com/drbasaria/
https://drbasaria.com/

Dr. Basaria is a transformational health expert and National Board-Certified Health and Wellness Coach, blending Eastern and Western medicine to promote holistic well-being. She holds dual Master's degrees in Biochemistry and Health Promotion, a Doctorate in Public Health Practice, and certifications as a yoga teacher and meditation guide. Her approach integrates scientific evidence with a mind-body-soul methodology, addressing chronic conditions by fostering physical health, mental peace, emotional joy, and spiritual vibrancy. Inspired by the loss of her mother to diabetes at 52 and her own prediabetes diagnosis in her late 30s, Dr. Basaria overcame her condition through transformative lifestyle changes. She has since dedicated her career to empowering individuals to prevent and reverse chronic disease through sustainable habits. Her mission is to help clients achieve vibrant health, overcome stress, and align their lives with their core values for lasting happiness and fulfillment.

# The Journey to My Core

By Neelofer Basaria, DrPH

In a few months, I will be turning 50. As I approach this milestone in my life, I find myself standing at a crossroads of reflection and revelation. Living half a century has given me experiences that shaped who I am today. There have been moments of joy so bright they radiated my entire being, and times of deep despair that felt endless. Throughout these years, I have worked on my physical, mental, and emotional health, yet it wasn't until I discovered that true fulfillment, peace, and balance only started to make sense to me when I started to connect with my inner self—my spiritual core. By tuning into that quiet but powerful voice inside, I unearthed what really matters. This chapter is a story of that journey and the lessons I learned along the way.

From as far back as I can remember, as a young girl, I dreamed of becoming a doctor. I was fascinated by the idea of healing people and being a source of comfort and support to them during their most testing moments. Yet, when the time came to decide my path for the future, instead of opting for medical school, I found myself drawn toward studying human genetics and biology, solving the mysteries of life at a molecular level. My journey led me to a master's degree in biochemistry, where I got a chance to gain a detailed understanding of the workings of the human body at a cellular level. This knowledge became the foundation for a career dedicated to understanding health and disease.

After graduating with a double master's degree in biochemistry and health promotion, I started working at the most prestigious breast cancer foundation. My work there allowed me to assess the impact of funding programs on breast cancer research. While I was pleased with my contributions to the larger picture of cancer research, I longed for something more personal—a one-on-one connection with the people whose lives were touched by the disease.

While I was still working on my graduate studies, life introduced me to loss in an extremely personal way. My mother, who was diagnosed late with diabetes, was rapidly overcome by its complications. I watched her endure the devastating consequences—kidney failure, amputation, vision loss, and heart failure—until she passed away at the age of 52. I was in my 20s, and her death felt like a part of me had been ripped away. Being by her side during her illness brought us closer than ever, and losing her was like losing a piece of my own identity.

Years later, after her passing, as a young mother, I was diagnosed with pre-diabetes, as I carried strong genetic markers for the disease. I resolved not to let history repeat itself. Armed with my knowledge of human biology, I worked diligently to reverse the diagnosis. I adopted mindful eating, shed excess weight, and made significant lifestyle changes. However, the physical improvements were not mirrored by my inner state. Stress consumed me as I juggled the demands of family life, volunteer work, a doctoral program in public health practice, and multiple responsibilities—including working two jobs at school. My inner self—the very core of my being—was suffocating under the weight of external expectations.

My body began to bear the brunt of this neglect. I developed sciatica and hypertension, and my doctor informed me that my back had aged twenty years beyond my biological age. Chronic pain became a constant companion, leading to a back surgery that marked a turning point in my life. I was desperate for relief, and in that, I turned to yoga before and after my surgery. In my practice of yoga and meditation, I found the seeds of healing—not just physical but spiritual as well.

After earning my doctoral degree, I joined a major health insurance company as a data scientist. As part of my work there, I conducted large-scale population studies and behavioral health analyses. Yet, despite the professional success, I felt hollow from within. People had become data points in my spreadsheets, and my soul craved a deeper connection. The young girl who had once dreamed of comforting others had grown into a professional lost in data and reports, longing to touch lives directly. I was alive but not truly living, burdened by the incongruence between my work and the inner fire that urged me to make a tangible difference in people's lives.

That fire led me to a health coaching program, which became the catalyst for my transformation. I finally listened to my soul's whispers for the first time. I began to nurture my inner being, immersing myself in the study of yoga, meditation, and spirituality. It taught me that I am enough, that I don't need to prove myself to others to claim my self-worth, and that I don't need to say yes to things that make sense on the surface but conflict with my core identity. Slowly, I reclaimed my life. I learned to say no to things that drained me and yes to the pursuits that aligned with my values and desires.

I honored my needs, respected my boundaries, redefined my inner dialogue, spoke to myself with kindness, and affirmed my worth. I took time to nurture my body, mind, and soul by eating foods that nourished me, resting when I was tired, finding learning opportunities in my setbacks, and engaging in activities that brought me joy. As I listened to my soul's wisdom and walked the path it laid, I found myself attracting deeper connections and profound love. My work shifted from numbers to people as I began coaching women, helping them achieve health goals, reverse chronic conditions, and discover their own vitality. My academic knowledge, coupled with my personal experiences, came together seamlessly, enabling me to do what I do now professionally—coach women into living their most vibrant, authentic lives.

The journey to my core has been shaped by several practices that I now hold sacred. These are the lessons I share with you in the hope that they may illuminate your path toward peace, joy, and fulfillment:

1. **Joy as Your Compass**
   Joy fuels the soul and lights the way to your core. For me, dancing has been transformative—it instantly connects me to my inner energy,

filling me with childlike happiness. Joy is not a luxury but a necessity. Another key to joy for me is practicing gratitude. By focusing intentionally on my blessings—relationships, health, and even life's challenges—I've cultivated a mindset of abundance and positivity.

2. **Releasing Negative Energy**

Creating space for growth requires releasing negativity. Journaling, allowing myself to cry, and sharing vulnerabilities with trusted friends and family are my go-to methods for cleansing the mind and emotions. These practices create room for light and deeper connection.

3. **Introspection and Connecting to the Core**

Connecting with nature and meditating help me access my core. My outdoor walks remind me of my oneness with the universe, while the practice of meditation offers the stillness to detach from distractions, hear my soul's whispers, and align with my true self.

Today, as I am writing these words, I am not merely existing—I am thriving. I have learned and given priority to honoring my true self, to nurturing my soul as much as my body and mind. This alignment has brought me the fulfillment I once thought unattainable. To every woman who is reading this: You are a wellspring and a fountain of love, creativity, and strength. When you connect with your inner core, you unlock the potential to inspire, nurture, and transform the world around you.

Let us choose to live authentically by embracing our inner light and spreading it to those around us. In doing so, we reclaim not only our lives but also the infinite joy and peace that lie within.

## Jennifer Jenkins

Founder of Rooted Holistic Health Coaching

https://www.linkedin.com/in/jennifer-jenkins-rn-chc-fns-ryt-nlp-practitioner-1103825/
https://www.facebook.com/jejenkins1/
https://www.instagram.com/jen_jenkins_health_coach/
https://rootedholistichealth.com/

Jennifer Jenkins is a renowned leader in holistic wellness, dedicated to empowering individuals to reclaim their health and unlock their full potential. As a Registered Nurse, Health Coach, and Entrepreneur, Jennifer's mission is rooted in her own transformative healing journey, which led her to found Rooted Holistic Health Coaching. With over 25 years of experience, she specializes in addressing the root causes of metabolic imbalances, helping hundreds of clients break through limiting beliefs and restore optimal health.

Her unique approach goes beyond traditional methods, incorporating mindset shifts, nutrition, and holistic practices to achieve lasting results. Jennifer's programs are designed to address the body, mind, and spirit, providing a comprehensive solution to wellness.

As a sought-after speaker and workshop leader, she continues to inspire and guide others toward abundance and well-being in all aspects of life. Jennifer is committed to helping clients optimize their health and live vibrantly.

# From Darkness to Light: Reclaiming Your Health, Rewriting Your Story

By Jennifer Jenkins

I used to believe that giving everything to others—my patients, my kids, my family—was what made me a good mother, a good nurse, a good person. But what I didn't realize was that I was sacrificing myself in the process. I worked long hours in the hospital, pouring my energy into my patients, only to come home utterly depleted. My children and husband got the leftovers of me—exhausted, irritable, and running on fumes. Self-care wasn't even in my vocabulary.

At first, I ignored the warning signs. Fatigue, brain fog, weight fluctuations, inflammation, gut issues, chronic pain—just part of life, right? But as the years went on, my body began screaming for attention. I found myself sitting in doctor's offices month after month, desperately seeking answers. Each new specialist gave me a **new diagnosis**, a **new prescription**, and a **new label** for what was wrong with me. Before I knew it, I was taking a **cabinet full of medications** and juggling appointments with **eight different specialists**. Despite following all the medical advice, I wasn't getting better. In fact, I was getting worse.

I spent **five years** chasing a solution, spending **tens of thousands of dollars** trying to reclaim my health, only to feel more broken than ever. My rock bottom moment came when I realized I couldn't keep living like this—I didn't even know if I'd be around for my children or my husband. That thought shattered me. **Something had to change.**

And in that moment, I made a decision that changed everything.

Instead of looking outward for the next expert, the next medication, the next diagnosis—I turned **within**. I asked myself:

*What if the power to heal was within me all along?*

*What if I stopped focusing on what was wrong with me and started focusing on what I needed to heal?*

That shift—from victim to creator—was the turning point.

## Taking Back Control: My Healing Journey

I embarked on a journey to heal naturally—focusing on the root cause rather than just symptoms. Immersing myself in functional medicine, nutrition, neuroscience, energy healing, yoga, breathwork, and alternative therapies, I pursued over 20 certifications in holistic health alongside my nursing degree. My mission was to understand the body through multiple lenses, bridging science with ancient wisdom. I became my own experiment, systematically addressing every aspect of my health—layer by layer.

**Nutrition** – I stopped eating for convenience and started eating with intention for **cellular healing**, removing inflammatory foods and focusing on whole, nutrient-dense foods that fueled my body.

**Sleep & Recovery** – I prioritized **deep, restorative sleep**, focused on regulating for circadian rhythm, understanding that my body couldn't heal without proper rest. I optimized my sleep environment, implemented **nervous system regulation techniques**, and saw my energy skyrocket.

**Nervous System Healing** – Chronic stress had kept me in **fight-or-flight mode** for years. I learned how to **regulate my nervous system** through breathwork, meditation, and grounding techniques.

**Emotional Healing** – I did deep work with **Neuro-Linguistic Programming (NLP)** to release stored trauma, rewire subconscious beliefs, and break free from old emotional patterns that had been keeping me sick.

**Movement & Exercise** – Instead of punishing my body with excessive workouts, I focused on **functional movement**, strength training, yoga, and intuitive exercise that supported my body rather than depleted it.

**Mindset & Self-Talk** – I stopped identifying as a **sick person** and started identifying as a **healthy, thriving woman that was healing**. I realized that our **thoughts shape our reality**, and I actively rewrote the narrative I had been telling myself.

**Environment**- A crucial part of my healing was transforming my **environment**. I distanced myself from negative, energy-draining relationships and instead surrounded myself with people who embodied the health and lifestyle I aspired to. This shift reinforced positive habits, strengthened my mindset, and created a foundation for lasting transformation.

As a result, my energy **returned**, my body **began to heal**, and for the first time in my life—I wasn't just existing, **I was truly living and found my purpose.**

I showed up **better for my family, my patients, and myself.** The quality of my life improved **dramatically**, and I felt a sense of **empowerment I had never experienced before.**

## Shifting from Victim to Creator: The Power of Mindset & Science

This transformation wasn't just about physical changes—it was about shifting my **identity and mindset** at a deep level. Science confirms what ancient healing traditions have known for centuries:

- **Neuroplasticity** (the brain's ability to rewire itself) means that **you are never stuck**—you can change your thoughts, habits, and identity at any time.

- **Quantum physics** shows us that **where we place our focus, energy flows**—if you focus on disease, you reinforce it. If you focus on healing, you create the conditions for it.

- **Nervous system regulation** is key—when the body is in survival mode, healing is impossible. When we shift to **safety and relaxation**, the body can facilitate healing.

So how can you **reclaim your health, rewrite your story, and step into empowerment?** Here are the strategies that changed my life.

## 1. Reframe Your Self-Talk: Your Words Create Your Reality

**Victim language:**

> *"Why does this always happen to me?"*
> *"I'll never feel better."*
> *"I have (insert diagnosis), so this is just my life now."*

**Empowered language:**

> *"What is this challenge teaching me?"*
> *"What small step can I take toward healing today?"*
> *"I am actively healing, and my body is working with me."*

**Action Step:** Catch yourself when you use **disempowering language** and consciously **reframe it into possibility.**

## 2. Rewire Subconscious Patterns with NLP

Your subconscious mind controls **95% of your thoughts and behaviors.** If you have a deep-rooted belief of **"I'm not enough"** or **"I can't heal"**, your mind will seek evidence to prove it true.

**Action Step:** Use this NLP technique to **rewrite limiting beliefs:**

1. **Identify** a limiting belief (e.g., *"I'll never get better"*).

2. **Interrupt the pattern** (snap a rubber band on your wrist, say "Cancel!" out loud).

3.  **Replace it** with an empowering belief (*"My body is capable of healing"*).

4.  **Anchor it with emotion** (visualize a time you felt strong and powerful).

## 3. Regulate Your Nervous System for Deep Healing

Your nervous system controls healing, digestion, and immune function. When stuck in **chronic stress (fight-or-flight mode),** your body prioritizes survival over repair. To heal effectively, you must activate the **parasympathetic (rest-and-digest) state.**

### 1. Breathing: Reset Your Nervous System

Deep breathing signals safety to the brain. Use the **4-7-8 method**:

- Inhale for **four** seconds, hold for **seven**, and exhale for **eight** seconds.

- Repeat for **three to four minutes** several times a day.

### 2. Grounding: Reconnect with the Earth

Grounding balances the body's electrical charge, reducing inflammation and stress.

- Walk **barefoot on grass or sand** for **10–20 minutes daily.**

- If outdoors isn't an option, use a **grounding mat or sheets.**

### 3. Vagus Nerve Activation: Fast-Track Relaxation

Stimulating the **vagus nerve** reduces stress and supports healing.

- **Humming or chanting** activates relaxation.

- **Cold exposure** (cold face splash or shower) calms the nervous system.

- **Deep, rhythmic breathing** lowers stress hormones.

## 4. Meditation: Cultivate Inner Stillness

Just **5–10 minutes of meditation daily** can help rewire the brain for calm and healing.

- Try **guided meditation, body scans, or mindful walking** in nature.
- Use apps like **Calm or Insight Timer** to build consistency.

## Final Thought

Your body heals in a **state of relaxation.** Training your nervous system to feel safe is the key to **long-term health and transformation.**

# 4. Embody Your Future Self NOW

Your future self—the **healthy, thriving, vibrant you**—already exists. The key is to **start acting like her today.**

**Action Step:** Every morning, ask yourself:

*"What would the healthiest version of me do today?"*

Then **do it**—whether it's eating nourishing foods, setting boundaries, or prioritizing rest.

# Final Words: The Power to Heal Is Within You

I used to believe my health was out of my control. But the truth? **We have far more power than we've been led to believe.** When I stopped looking outside for answers and started taking responsibility for my healing, everything changed.

And now, **I'm here to tell you: You can, too.**

**You are not broken.**

**You are not a victim.**
**You are powerful beyond measure.**

The first step? **Decide.**

## You Are More Powerful Than You've Ever Been Made to Believe

Everything you need to heal, transform, and thrive is already within you. You were never meant to live in limitation—you were designed for vitality, abundance, and purpose. Every day, I help my clients uncover this truth, break free from what's holding them back, and step into the life they were destined for. Now, it's your turn. No more waiting. No more doubting. The power to heal and create the life you desire has been inside you all along.

I will believe in you until you believe in yourself. But the truth is—you already have everything you need. The only thing left is to take the first step. If you're ready to reclaim your health or break free from limiting beliefs that have been holding you back and step into your highest potential, I invite you to walk this path with me. You don't have to do it alone. Visit www.RootedHolisticHealth.com to connect with me—your transformation starts now.

## Tammy Gibson

Tough Like Tammy
Speaker

https://www.linkedin.com/in/toughliketammy/
https://www.facebook.com/ToughLikeTammy/
https://www.instagram.com/toughliketammy
https://www.toughliketammy.com/

Tammy Gibson is a dynamic speaker, consultant, and amputee advocate who empowers professional women to transform their challenges into their greatest strengths. After a life-altering journey of limb loss and a four-month hospital stay due to COVID-19, Tammy turned adversity into a mission to uplift and inspire others. Her story of resilience, perseverance, and grace is a testament to the power of embracing life's toughest moments as opportunities for growth. With a background as a fashion blogger turned personal growth advocate, Tammy guides women to harness their inner strength, build authentic personal brands, and lead with unapologetic confidence. Her transformative sessions provide practical tools to navigate adversity, amplify leadership, and create meaningful impact in both career and personal life. Tammy's mission is clear: to help professional women unlock their potential, lead with purpose, and turn resilience into a powerful force for success and joy.

# Resilient and Radiant:
# Owning Your Path to Wellness

By Tammy Gibson

I turned 50 in the summer of 2021. That same summer, I began my health journey, losing nine pounds, gaining strength with Pilates classes three times a week, and, most importantly, improving my mental health. For the first time in a decade, I prioritized my well-being—and I felt amazing. This foundation of health became a lifeline when, on October 24, 2021, I went to the ER with extremely weak legs.

I returned home four months later, having faced a diagnosis of A-Typical COVID-19. My journey out of the hospital was marked by profound loss and immense challenges: my right leg was amputated above the knee, I had nerve damage in both hands, a Stage 4 kidney injury requiring dialysis, and the soleus muscle was removed from my left calf. Despite these setbacks, I believe that prioritizing my health earlier that year saved my life. Wellness and self-care, quite literally, gave me a second chance.

After returning home in February 2022, I began working to regain my strength and health. My kidneys have healed to Stage 1, and I am no longer on dialysis. I've relearned to walk, started to workout at the gym, and resumed private Pilates lessons in my home. Feeling healthier and stronger, I've rebuilt my stamina to relaunch my online business and share my story as a speaker, emphasizing the power of resilience.

When life threw me into the depths of uncertainty, it also handed me an opportunity to reclaim my glow. My journey included months where dialysis dictated my existence. Early morning appointments and exhausting treatments drained my body and spirit. Yet amidst the chaos, there was hope.

## Taking Ownership of Wellness

Faced with Stage 4 kidney injury, I was determined to flip the script. My husband and I sought out the best kidney expert in town, diving deep into research and crafting a comprehensive plan to nurture my kidneys back to health. It was a lifestyle overhaul: a low-protein, low-sodium, low-potassium diet, creatine for muscle repair, and an extraordinary amount of water. I even tuned into binaural beats for kidney healing during my daily naps. Slowly but surely, the tides turned. Over 18 months, my kidneys improved from Stage 4 to Stage 1, a transformation my doctor called miraculous.

I give all glory to God for my healing and recognize that putting in the work and taking ownership of my situation were essential steps in rewriting my story. Establishing a foundation of good health has taught me that wellness is essential to resilience. Whether facing personal challenges or supporting others, being in optimal health helps us think clearly, navigate adversity, and create a foundation for comebacks.

## Empower Your Wellness Journey

Imagine standing at a crossroads, knowing you have the power to take control of your life and steer it toward vitality and joy. Wellness begins with this realization: You are in charge. Pause to reflect on your current state. What parts of your life need attention? Be honest with yourself because awareness is the first step toward meaningful change.

As you take stock, open your mind to possibilities. Wellness is not one-size-fits-all. Explore solutions that resonate with you—a new fitness routine, mindfulness practice, or nutritional adjustments. Trust your instincts and dare to try new approaches.

Once you have a vision for change, make a plan. Picture it as a map guiding you toward a healthier, more vibrant life. Break it into manageable steps and take them with confidence. Each small action builds momentum.

And as you move forward, remember that consistency is your ally. Even on challenging days, your dedication will carry you closer to your goals.

Lean on the people who uplift and inspire you. Wellness is not a solo journey. Surround yourself with loved ones, mentors, or a supportive community. Let their encouragement fuel your resilience and remind you that you're never alone in this endeavor.

Celebrate yourself every step of the way. Each milestone, no matter how small, reinforces your strength and keeps you motivated. Wellness is a journey of empowerment, and each success illuminates the path ahead.

## Finding Strength in the Glow

The glow that comes from wellness and self-care is transformative. It's a light that shines from within, fueled by the confidence and joy of knowing you're prioritizing yourself. And that light is a reflection of God's grace working through you. Nourish your body with foods that energize you, move in ways that bring you happiness, and hydrate to sustain your vitality. Quiet your mind through mindfulness practices like meditation, journaling, or simply breathing deeply. Feed your spirit with activities that resonate with your soul, whether it's prayer, creativity, or time in nature.

Set boundaries that honor your needs. Protect your energy and prioritize what truly matters. Above all, celebrate yourself, not as an act of pride, but as a way to honor the life and strength God has given you. Revel in the power of feeling vibrant, focused, and healthy. This is your gift to yourself and a testament to His faithfulness, and it's one worth cherishing every day.

## Conclusion: Make It Happen

Reflecting on my journey from kidney failure to healing, I am deeply grateful for the lessons learned. Wellness is not a destination but a journey—one that requires intention, action, and perseverance. By embracing self-care, you not only transform your health but also rediscover your glow.

It's your turn to take ownership of your story. Whether you're facing health challenges, career hurdles, or personal struggles, remember that you hold the power to create a life of vitality and joy. Assess your situation, explore solutions, and commit to the steps that will help you thrive.

Incorporating wellness and self-care saved my life. It can transform yours too. Let your story inspire others and create a ripple effect of empowerment and wellness. Together, we can shine brightly and illuminate the path for others to follow.

## Marissa Elyse Rowles

The Chrysalis Coach
Holistic Health & Lifestyle Coach

https://www.facebook.com/the.chrysalis.coach
https://www.instagram.com/the.chrysalis.coach
https://www.thechrysaliscoach.com

Marissa is a dedicated wellness coach and healer with a passion for guiding individuals on their journey to becoming their most aligned and empowered selves. With a deep understanding of the challenges faced by empathetic and sensitive individuals, she emphasizes self-care as an essential foundation for balance and resilience. Drawing on extensive training in holistic wellness, trauma-informed practices, and energy healing, Marissa blends practical strategies with intuitive insight to support deep transformation. Her unique approach bridges science, spirituality, and self-awareness, creating a safe space for growth and renewal.  Through her work, Marissa teaches clients to honor their needs, embrace their worth, and cultivate practices that sustain their physical, emotional, and spiritual well-being. She empowers others to set boundaries and prioritize themselves without guilt, fostering healing from within. A lifelong learner and advocate for intentional living, Marissa inspires clients to design lives rooted in purpose and joy.

# Choosing Self-Care Over Self-Sacrifice

By Marissa Elyse Rowles

A few years ago, my life reached a pivotal moment—the kind that forces you to reassess your values and realign your priorities. I had been living out of alignment for years, chasing superficial goals. I was obsessed with work and filled with excitement over expanding my income while building my career. For several years, I worked a minimum of 65–70 hours a week (always while enrolled in classes or certifications on the side) and often only slept about five hours each night.

At the time, I had just transitioned from freelancing to my first full-time salaried job. The stability of a regular paycheck felt like I had finally accomplished the security I needed. But no matter how hard I worked or how many hours I clocked, my wallet wasn't getting heavier. I was surrounded by peers with family-provided nest eggs that reinforced my own feelings of scarcity.

I became desperate to work more hours, to prove myself, and to overcome my deep-seated feelings of needing to catch up. On the surface, it looked like I was working hard, but in reality, I was unconsciously trying to fit in with a group of people whose values were out of alignment with my own.

Unlike the other women I was around, I didn't spend much on myself—only if I saw it beneficial to elevate my career. Self-care or slow weekends away wasn't even a consideration. I couldn't justify taking a moment off (let alone just for myself) because I had such an ingrained belief that the more I worked, the more it would equate to freedom. Unconsciously, I was living as though my entire self-worth depended entirely on what I could achieve.

This skewed lifestyle continued for about a year until I found myself on the opposite side of the country in an even more intense corporate setting. The pace and pressure of this new role (alongside trying to balance a second job) pushed me to the edge, forcing me to confront the reality that I couldn't keep doing what I was doing. I had to face the harm it was doing to my health from being obsessed every day with working. I was so worn out and chronically stressed that I couldn't even see that the thing I had convinced myself was a path to success—was leading to my undoing.

I told myself that overworking was benefitting me, that it was the price of building toward my dream life, but in reality, it was bringing me more chronic stress and sinking me deeper into levels of exhaustion. The harder I pushed, the less fulfilled I felt, and the more disconnected I became—not just from my goals, but from myself.

It shouldn't come as a surprise that my lack of sleep and delayed burnout caught up with me–eventually, I was let go. All the years I'd spent working so hard seemed to be for nothing, and there I was, with no motivation, no energy, and no spark.

I knew it was time for me to have a new approach. I knew it was time for me to seek answers and ones that could only be found by turning inwards. Luckily, I saw stopping my overworking cycle as an invitation—a chance to pause and uncover the deeper roots of my behavior. I realized my reasons for neglecting myself stemmed from something much deeper, something that must have been rooted in childhood conditioning.

## Inherited Patterns for Overgiving

I was raised in a family of four, where both of my parents served as primary caretakers for my older brother with special needs (he has Down Syndrome, Autism, and OCD). From a young age, I witnessed them pour themselves endlessly into someone else's life. Because of his challenges and need for constant supervision, they were left with little time or energy to indulge in self-care or any significant personal pursuits. I remember my parents only prioritizing one exclusive vacation.

As I began to focus on my own healing, I realized I had inherited several limiting beliefs: that my worth was tied to how much I could give and that my own needs weren't a priority. Slowly, I began to shift my mindset, reminding myself that self-care wasn't selfish—it was essential. My perception of needing to self-sacrifice for success had to go.

## It's Not Indulgence, It's Alignment

Over time, I realized that self-care isn't about indulgence; it's about alignment. It's about creating a life that reflects your values and nurturing the parts of you that fuel your inner glow. For me, that meant prioritizing rest, and trusting that the more I invested in my wellness, the more success would come as a result.

I began making small but meaningful changes. I started saying no to commitments that drained me and practiced asking for help. I redefined my meaning of success, letting go of the guilt I once felt when I put myself first. Instead of seeing self-care as an indulgence, I reframed it as a necessity.

I stopped equating my value with productivity and embraced the idea that rest was a critical part of my success. The more I invested in myself—physically, emotionally, and mentally—the more I noticed a shift. My energy returned, my creativity flowed, and opportunities that aligned with my true self started to appear.

Self-care, I realized, is about creating a life that feels good to live. It's about nourishing your body, tending to your heart, and aligning your actions with your values. When you prioritize yourself, you not only rejuvenate your spirit but also become magnetic to the experiences and relationships you desire.

Reclaiming your glow doesn't require an overnight transformation. It's about making intentional choices that honor your worth. Start small: listen to your body, say no when something feels wrong, and carve out space for rest. Trust that the more you care for yourself, the brighter you'll shine—and that light will ripple out, inspiring others to do the same.

# Cara McGregor

Cariad Coaching Pty Ltd

https://www.linkedin.com/in/cariadcoaching/
https://www.facebook.com/profile.php?id=100091581413795
https://www.cariadcoaching.com.au
https://www.cariadcoaching.com.au/nonverbal

Cara is a powerhouse Mindset and Transformational Confidence Coach, a dynamic Speaker, and an expert in Non-Verbal Communication and Influence. She's here to make you believe in your ability to conquer anything by aligning your mind and body for unstoppable results. But there's more—Cara's a wife, animal lover, fierce advocate, and a fun-loving firecracker. Having faced life's toughest challenges—beating cancer, navigating divorce, and moving across the globe in one whirlwind year—she's transformed her trials into practical confidence strategies that energize and inspire. From corporate workshops to one-on-one coaching, Cara combines mindset mastery with body language brilliance to help people unlock their full potential. Her unique leadership training, blending coaching with horse interaction, revolutionizes non-verbal communication skills. Empowering women to embrace their unapologetic selves, Cara's infectious energy and empathetic nature will leave you ready to take on the world—and win.

# From Cancer to Courage –
# Embracing Positive Movement,
# Body Language, and Nature

By Cara McGregor

In 2006, I was due to emigrate from the UK to Australia to start a new adventure. The excitement was building when in February, my world stopped. I found a lump in my breast. I had breast cancer. I was 32. I was fit and healthy, this was not possible! Within days, I was undergoing a mastectomy and grappling with the harsh reality of chemotherapy and intravenous treatments that would dominate the next two years of my life. My body felt alien, my confidence shattered, and my life—as a woman, wife, and horse trainer—was utterly upended.

But this chapter isn't about the pain; it's about the path out of it—a path that was shaped by movement, nature, and the silent strength of positive body language.

## The Body Betrayed

Cancer doesn't just invade your cells; it invades your sense of self. Losing my breast and long blonde hair felt like losing pieces of my identity. My husband's refusal to engage emotionally added to the isolation. Even my family's response left me feeling more alone than ever. By the time my treatment ended, I was a shadow of my former self—physically and emotionally.

As the walls closed in, I sought solace in the one constant in my life: movement. It wasn't graceful or even intentional at first. It was just about surviving another day. But each small step reminded me that my body, though battered, was still mine to command.

## Movement as Medicine

In late 2007, I hit rock bottom, I was close to finishing my intravenous treatment, and I ended my marriage—it hadn't been a positive place for a long time, and this was the third time I had tried to leave. As I left this final time, he yelled at me, "I don't understand, you don't have anything, how can that be better than being here with me?" No home, no job, and no self-esteem. But I still managed to muster the response that I felt in my core, "The grass may not be greener on the other side, but I can mow it when I like!" I was tired, but there was still a flicker of flame inside, which was being crushed, and I knew I had to leave.

Life has a way of showing us a crack of light when we least expect it. That light came during a skiing trip where I supported partially sighted children. Watching them glide down the slopes with unrestrained joy and trust—despite their limitations—was a revelation. It reminded me of the resilience of the human spirit and the profound connection between movement and healing.

Skiing demanded my presence and focus. I couldn't wallow in fear or doubt on those slopes. I had to engage fully with the moment. This shift—from fear to engagement—sparked something inside me. Movement wasn't just a physical act; it was an emotional release, a reconnection to life's flow.

## The Language of the Body

Cancer silenced my voice in many ways, but it also taught me the power of how your body movement, posture, and energy can influence your state of mind, and even those around you. Horses played a pivotal role in this lesson. As a horse trainer, I had always known that horses communicate primarily through body language. They respond to subtle shifts in posture, energy, and intention. When I approached Oska, my horse, with tension or fear, he mirrored it back to me. But when I centred myself, softened my movements, allowed myself to be in the moment, and exuded calm confidence, he responded with trust and connection, as had the many horses I had trained over the years. Now, I saw it from another perspective.

This dynamic taught me that body language isn't just about how others see us; it's about how we feel about ourselves. Slumped shoulders, hesitant steps, and a downward gaze reflected my inner turmoil. Yet, as I started to rebuild, I realized that changing my body language could reshape my mental state.

Body language is a two-way street. The way you hold yourself not only influences how others perceive you but also impacts how you feel about yourself. I began standing taller, even when I didn't feel strong. I made relaxed eye contact, even when I felt invisible. I smiled, even when my heart ached. These small shifts weren't about faking confidence; they were about claiming it and learning to feel it again.

Understanding body language helped me regain control over how I interacted with the world. When I projected confidence through my posture, movements, and expressions, I noticed people responding to me differently—with more respect, warmth, and openness. This positive feedback loop became a powerful tool in rebuilding my self-esteem and strengthening my mindset.

Your physiology—the way you carry your body—is intricately tied to your psychology. When you change your posture, you also shift your emotional state. Standing tall with your shoulders back signals not only to others but also to your brain that you are capable and strong. These intentional changes helped me feel more in control, even on days when life felt overwhelming.

## Nature's Embrace

Nature became my sanctuary. After my treatments, I found comfort in long walks, surrounded by the rhythm of the natural world. There's a unique healing power in the rustle of leaves, the splash of waves on the beach, the warmth of the sun, and the steady companionship of a horse. My horse, Oska, was a constant through my darkest days, and he still is. His calm presence and unwavering trust mirrored the steadiness I longed to find within myself.

Horses, much like humans, respond to energy and intention. They are natural teachers of non-verbal communication and how your body language can influence you and those around you. This dynamic taught me the importance of aligning my internal state with my external actions. It wasn't just about surviving anymore; it was about thriving in harmony with myself and the world around me.

## Building Courage One Step at a Time

In late 2008, I took the biggest leap of my life. Armed with two bags and a one-way ticket to Australia, I set out to rebuild my life from scratch. Those first weeks were terrifying. I was truly alone, knowing no one and carrying the weight of my past like an invisible backpack.

But Australia offered something precious: space. Space to breathe, to think, and to redefine who I was. I started with small steps—house-sitting jobs that kept me moving and allowed me to meet new people. Each new connection felt like a lifeline, and gradually, I began to trust in the process of rebuilding.

## Reclaiming Identity Through Movement

Exercise became a cornerstone of my recovery—not for weight loss or fitness, but for the sheer joy of movement. I did a little of everything jogging, bush walking, swimming, yoga, and of course, horse riding, savouring the ways my body could still serve me. Movement reminded me of my agency, my strength, and my capacity to heal.

Nature, too, played an integral role. I spent hours outside, soaking in the beauty of the Australian landscape. Whether it was walking along the coast or riding through the bush, each moment in nature felt like a dialogue with the universe—one that reassured me I was part of something vast and resilient.

## The Power of Positive Body Language

Rebuilding wasn't just about physical movement; it was about healing and reprogramming my mindset. I consciously adopted a posture of confidence, that relaxed steadfast confidence I learned from mirroring the horses, taking each step with a steady determination no matter what was in front of me. Even on days when I felt anything but strong, this practice helped me embody the strength I wanted to reclaim.

Positive body language also transformed my interactions. People respond to what you project. By carrying myself with assurance, I began to attract supportive, uplifting connections. This cycle of projecting and receiving positivity became a cornerstone of my new life.

## A New Chapter

Today, my life is unrecognizable from those dark days. I'm remarried to a wonderful man, living on a farm we designed together. Oska made the journey to Australia, a steadfast reminder of the life I've rebuilt. Through coaching, I help others navigate their own journeys of transformation, sharing the lessons I've learned about resilience, movement, and self-reclamation.

My journey from cancer to courage wasn't linear or easy. It was a mosaic of small choices—to move, to connect, to stand tall. Each choice brought me closer to the life I live today. If there's one thing I've learned, it's that healing starts with a choice. The body, mind, and spirit are deeply interconnected, and by nurturing one, we can uplift them all.

For anyone facing their own trials, I offer this: find your movement, claim your body language, and immerse yourself in nature. These simple yet profound acts hold the power to transform even the darkest of journeys into a pathway of light and possibility. The other side of the storm is waiting for you, stronger and brighter than you can imagine.

## Carmen K. Maendel

Nate's Property Maintenance LLC
Co-Owner & Business Office Manager

https://www.linkedin.com/in/carmen-maendel-17510944/
https://www.facebook.com/ncmaendel
https://www.instagram.com/maendelcarmen/
https://natespropertymaintenance.com/
https://www.facebook.com/profile.php?id=100093303554586

Hello I'm Carmen Maendel. Nate and I are a husband and wife team. Our fifteen year old son, Josh officially works for our company as well. We have embarked upon an entrepreneurial journey together that is extremely rewarding for all of us. We own and operate Nate's Property Maintenance LLC together. I handle the business on the home front while my husband coordinates our projects on the job sites with our clients and team of workers. We compliment each other very well working together, and remain very service oriented in our company. Some of the business roles I perform are the following: balancing our books, scheduling our clients, regularly posting to social media, arranging purchase contracts for new business equipment, keeping our business licenses and registration up to date, documenting client files, and much more. Nate coordinates all the equipment on the job sites and carefully plans for each of our projects we do.

# When Her Cup Runneth Over

By Carmen K. Maendel

## Introduction: My Identity in Jesus Christ

Hello, Beautiful! My name is Carmen Maendel, and I am a child of God. I rededicated my life to Jesus Christ on November 4, 2006, after coming to the Lord at the very young age of thirteen. God has worked in amazing ways in the areas of fitness and nutrition and overall wellness and self-care in both my personal and professional life. I have an immense passion for this topic and devoted eight years of my life to training more than fifty women in our Maendel Fitness gym. God has guided and directed me every step of the way, from my initial certification of CFT and later Master's level in Nutrition, Precision Nutrition, and DNA Testing and Analysis to the process of acquiring each piece of equipment of the gym. I have prayed over every little and big decision involved in running our gym and spa. I was blessed with both the opportunity to do some sports and fitness modeling and become a founding member of the Men's Health Fitness Council in March 2017. My goal is to share with you as many golden nuggets of fitness and nutrition knowledge and information for you to use and apply to your everyday life for wellness and self-care.

## My Story: From Dim to Radiant and Glowing

A woman glows when she is loved, cared for, appreciated, feels useful to others, and is working in an area she is deeply passionate about. All women are beautiful regardless of their size, body type, or bone structure. Confidence is feeling amazing with the body God blessed you with, and respecting your body as the temple of the Holy Spirit. Confidence is your identity in Jesus Christ and not a number on a scale. It's all about rockin' what you got! I did not always have high energy and exuberate great levels of confidence, as I do today when I walk into a room. When I was a freshman at Cornell College, I was away from home for the first time and had terrible eating and exercise habits. I lived off vending machines and pizza during late-night crunches for writing papers and completing projects due the following day. My father was battling cancer, and my best friend crossed the center line, hitting another vehicle head-on. She miraculously survived; however, her little brother and fiancé did not. This was a very difficult time for me in life, and all my relationships suffered. I started to spiral down in a very unhealthy way. I knew I did not want to live like this forever, and I did something about it.

I began to run at the gym and get involved with as many sports activities at the college as I could with my sorority or with friends at that time. I started avoiding the vending machines or late-night pizza and paid attention to the food I ate at the cafeteria. The weight began to come off, and I started to feel healthier again. After college, I began working out regularly at the 24-Hour Fitness Gym and paying closer attention to my diet and exercise in general. One of the strategies I used for myself and my clients was the 80/20 Philosophy. Eighty percent of the time, pay close attention to what you eat and exercise, and twenty percent of the time, take a break from working out and eat what you like, in moderation. Moderation is the key to being able to eat whatever you like whenever you want. As long as you eat smaller portions, you can enjoy some of your favorite foods that may have heavier fats, carbs, and sugars in them.

## Maendel Fitness: Founding the Company in 2016–2023

I began to view diet and exercise as a lifestyle. If you do something 21 days in a row successfully, it can start to become a habit. If you continue with healthy habits making small tweaks here and there, it can become your lifestyle. As I learned all this amazing health and fitness information, I was passionate to learn even more and share it with others. After heavy prayer, I decided to open Maendel Fitness in 2016 after I achieved my Certified Fitness Trainer licensure with ISSA. I started helping my clients, all-encompassing with a broad scope of the following: 1) Core Work, 2) HIIT Training, 3) Strength Training, and 4) Spiritual and Mind/Body Connection. We looked at Limiting Factors that may be standing in the way of them achieving their goals. Together, we put a plan together to help them break through some of the fears and barriers they had that were keeping them from achieving their fitness and nutrition goals. I also encouraged my clients to choose a Bible verse that they related to and were passionate about and recite it three times in the morning and evening. Writing affirmations and reciting them daily was also part of the program I created for myself earlier on and used with clients as well. We used SMART Goals and set three twelve-week goals together in the areas of fitness and nutrition. Through client feedback over the years, I realized how important it was for them to recite out loud the goals they had for themselves each day, three times in the morning and evening.

With God's guidance, I experienced major breakthroughs with my clients in the areas of confidence boosting and realizing they were capable of way more than they thought they were. I had them write out "I can" statements and affirmations on paper and recite those as well. It was incredible to witness them moving from tears and not being able to write down a single thing, into smiles and writing down a list of twenty-plus things they were capable of doing in our gym in a six-month period of time. I believed in the philosophy of "teaching them how to fish" instead of "giving them fish." This means that my desire was to have my clients graduate from my program, be able to create their own workout programs, and know their way around any gym they entered into. I pushed them to their limits; however, I do understand that everyone has a limited capacity they can reach. I was sensitive to this and always tried to set my clients up for success and not failure. I had a rule that I would never ask my client to do something that I would not be able and willing to do myself. This created an enormous amount of trust and respect between us and helped them reach incredible new levels of fitness.

God has blessed me with the experience of eight years working side by side with women helping them lose anywhere between twenty and sixty-plus pounds. I watched these women blossom into incredible, confident women. It was all-encompassing and not just about losing weight. I taught these women proper form in lifting weights and how to create their own HIIT Cardio and Strength Training workouts. I also have helped these same women with spiritual mind and bodywork as part of the nutrition training I did with them: teaching my clients information about health and nutrition, while challenging them to reach different goals and continuing to set them up for success, not failure, to achieve a true balance in lifestyle. I encouraged them to look at the spheres of influence in their lives and identify the things they had control of and the things they did not, and how to recognize the difference between the two. I also taught my clients that they did not have a problem with motivation; however, it was the discipline that they struggled with. If someone feels like doing something, they do it when they are motivated to do it. However, when someone does something, regardless of whether or not they feel like doing it, they are disciplined in that area. We can learn to discipline ourselves to be able to achieve various accomplishments in life.

For the rest of this chapter, I would love to provide you with some tangible tips, tricks, and resources that God has revealed to me so that you can use them to embrace your own wellness journey. I will be drawing from various parts of my online fitness and nutrition program Rock Hard Body - Power, Strength, Fitness that I created in 2023. The foundation I like to start with a client is the Spiritual component. I encouraged my clients to seek out their favorite Bible scripture and meditate on specific scriptures: Luke 18:27, Matthew 7:7, 1 Corinthians 2:9, Mark 11:23, Ephesians 4:23, Psalm 51:10, and Proverbs 3:5 are all part of that foundation. We also, throughout the upcoming sessions, talked about working out their muscle of prayer, the fruits of the spirit, and the power of daily journaling. When I first started training clients in 2016, I did not emphasize as much the spiritual mind and body connection; however, in the last several years of training clients, I did. I always encouraged in that direction, and if I felt any resistance at all, we would move away from it. I was surprised at how many of my clients in the last few years were very open to learning about the spiritual mind and body connection, and it helped them achieve their incredible fitness and nutrition results.

I established a baseline with them by measuring (neck, chest, waist, hips, right arm, right leg), weighing them with my bioelectrical scale percentages (weight, body fat, muscle, bone), measuring their height, and recording their body mass index (BMI), and taking before and after shots from the front, side, and back. We then sat down together and created three fitness goals and three nutrition twelve-week goals. I asked them to recite these three times in the morning and evening out loud. I also encouraged them to create positive affirmations and "I Can" statements reciting them out loud as well. As we progressed through the sessions, I taught them the proper form for lifting weights and how to use the various machines and exercise equipment in our gym. As we worked on core strength, I taught them that one of the best ways to alleviate back pain is to strengthen their core muscles. The back and core work together, so if you have a weak core, you probably also have a weak back. The reverse is true also, so if you have a strong core, you have a strong back. It is very important to incorporate Core Strength Training into your workouts.

I also taught them how to create a HIIT High-Intensity Interval Training portion of their workout. One easy 20–30 min HIIT workout could be the following: 3 min warm up—2 min HIIT followed by 1 min recovery—3 min cool down. Another one could be: 3 min warm up— 10 sec HIIT followed by 50 sec recovery—3 min cool down. You can get creative with the intervals of HIIT and recovery. When you work out with HIIT Cardio, your oxygen level is at a higher rate, and your body begins to repair itself. As your body cools down, your metabolism speeds up, and you burn more fat. HIIT Training is a very efficient way to exercise, and weight lifting is one component of HIIT Training. Why do we lift weights? The scientific reason why we lift weights is the following: building more muscle tissue increases your demand for glucose. The muscles pull glucose from your bloodstream so that your blood sugar levels do not rise to abnormal levels within your body. Recovery between sets, during workouts, between workout days, and on the weekends is very important when it comes to lifting weights.

God revealed to me through prayer that the spiritual mind and body connection is very important. I worked with clients with the mindset portion for fifteen minutes prior to training them for an hour in our gym. I taught them how to ditch their diet mentality and embrace healthy lifestyle choices for fitness and nutrition. Here are Five Ways to Embrace Change: 1) Seek out new perspectives and be teachable, 2) Do something new and exciting, stretching yourself out of your comfort zone, 3) Shed your old self and get rid of old negative habits, 4) Replace the bad habits with positive ones, and 5) Learn to live on faith and believe that good things are coming your way. Before we succeed in life, we first must be able to embrace change. Without change, growth is not possible. Forming good habits and being disciplined leads to feeling motivated; a huge transformation can then take place in your life. Here are a few examples of Healthy Lifestyle Choices: 1) Park farther away from your destination and walk, 2) Take the stairs over the elevator, 3) Get up and walk around for breaks regularly, 4) fitness program of HIIT Cardio, Strength Training, and Core Strength, 5) Emphasize core strength because a strong core leads to a strong body, 6) Get 6–8 hours of sleep daily, especially deep sleep, 7) Eliminate or decrease stress in your life, and 8) Drink at least 68 ounces of water throughout your day. Also, please don't hold on to the assumption that you can't grow and learn from past failures. You absolutely can learn from your past mistakes in life and be stronger moving forward. Most importantly, learn to operate and call upon God's strength and not your own.

Every obstacle you face offers an opportunity to improve. Pushing through challenging moments in life will help you reach a higher level. It may take us a while to accomplish something in life, but eventually, we will succeed if we keep on trying. We can choose how we respond to adversity in our lives. We may not be able to control what happens to us in life; however, we can choose how we respond to what happens to us. "You miss one hundred percent of the shots you don't take"—Burton W. Kanter; "You can't hit the ball (get a hit) if you don't swing (the bat)"—Wayne Gretzky. The definition of self-confidence is a feeling of trust in one's abilities, qualities, and judgment. What if a person has low self-esteem and lacks self-confidence? Self-confidence is a skill that can be learned, practiced, and perfected in life. Self-confidence is something that we can all learn to master, given lots of practice, perseverance, reliance, and full trust in God. Our identity is in Christ and not ourselves. We need to learn how to place the focus on Jesus and not on ourselves. When we do this, our self-confidence and peace in Christ will soar to new heights.

God has taught me about the need to have control in my life. Learning about the spheres of control can be helpful in breaking barriers and reaching for success in your fitness and nutrition goals. There are three categories of control: 1) Things you can control, 2) What you can influence, and 3) Everything else outside of your control and influence. Learn to recognize the difference between these three spheres of influence and have peace with the things that are completely out of your control. God is completely in control of everything in our lives at all times. If we learn to trust Him fully, we can give up that need for control in our lives and gain more peace. We also need to get rid of limiting factors in our life. There are false beliefs that are keeping you from crushing your goals and breaking through barriers in life. What are they? Some examples of limiting factors are the following: 1) Wishful thinking instead of doing the hard work, 2) Setting goals with unrealistic time frames, 3) Lack of planning or having systems in place to track your progress, 3) Lack of commitment or discipline and lack of perseverance and sustainability. Five Steps to Overcome These Limiting Factors: 1) Establish a solid foundation for your goals, 2) Set urgent but realistic time frames for goals, 3) Set yourself up for success with proper systems in place and tracking devices to monitor your progress, 4) Re-establish your "why" in life when your confidence decreases; then you can remind yourself why you are strongly committed to your goals, and 5) Set yourself up with success with a plan of consistent sustainability once you hit your goals, so you can maintain your progress for a lifetime. I was obedient to God's calling when He asked me to close Maendel Fitness and run Nate's Property Maintenance LLC alongside my husband. I feel blessed and honored to have gotten the eight years I did to work with and encourage women! Please feel free to use any of the resources I included for you below to help you achieve your ultimate fitness, nutrition, and wellness goals for self-care.

## Positive Biblical Affirmations:

- I am the Apple of His eye (Deuteronomy 32:10)
- I am Fearfully and Wonderfully made (Psalm 139:14)
- I am Kept in His perfect peace (Isaiah 26:3)
- I am an Overcomer (1 John 5:5)
- I am Redeemed (Ephesians 1:7)
- I am Yoked to a gentle Master (Matthew 11:29)
- I am the Temple of God the Holy Spirit (1 Corinthians 6:19)
- I am Purchased for God by the blood of Jesus (Revelation 5:9)
- I am Inseparable from the love of God in Christ Jesus (Romans 8:39)
- I am Loved with an everlasting Love (Jeremiah 31:3)
- I am Sealed with the Holy Spirit (Ephesians 1:13)
- I am Eternally secure (John 6:39)
- I am Chosen from before the foundation of the world (Ephesians 1:4)

- I am a New creation in Christ (2 Corinthians 5:17)
- I am a Daughter of the King (John 1:12)

## Maendel Fitness: Fitness & Nutrition Resources

- Carmen Maendel YouTube Channel
  https://www.youtube.com/@carmenmaendel6186

- MFC Muscle Menu
  https://drive.google.com/file/d/1iob0qnW2TLD8CE7cj9gLx9jP8hG1Jcfn/view?usp=sharing

- MFC Guru Grocery List
  https://drive.google.com/file/d/1FHt77_tiJostf7lEKNYzbeYTEqAG7i1L/view?usp=sharing

- MFC Tasty & Savory Cookbook
  https://drive.google.com/file/d/1RItKdZqlntip1Bh7AEzC67020xQmrJ_k/view?usp=sharing

- MFC Confidence Boost System
  https://drive.google.com/file/d/1wo7usMTuOzO1y3YHEglm-r7wnAydP7cv/view?usp=sharing

- MFC I Can Statements Worksheet
  https://drive.google.com/file/d/1oSLTWLCWLpdw6xQEWBIkd9D3IfBCSpG3/view?usp=sharing

## Helen Ross

The Well Life Lab
Nutritional Therapist

https://www.linkedin.com/in/helenrossthewelllifelab/
https://www.facebook.com/thewelllifelab
https://www.instagram.com/the_well_life_lab/
https://www.thewelllifelab.co.uk/

Helen Ross is a registered nutritionist and gut health specialist. She holds a BSc (Hons) in Nutritional Science and has worked as a nutritionist and cook for retreat companies, in addition to running her own business, The Well Life Lab. She provides personalised nutrition programmes, cooking workshops, and one-day retreats. Helen specialises in gut health and digestive disorders, including IBS, gluten disorders, and food intolerances, using a 'modified' low FODMAP approach and an anti-inflammatory diet. Her passion for nutrition stems from her own struggles with persistent gut issues, which led her to explore holistic solutions, which included lifestyle adjustments. She believes true gut health requires stress management, balanced nutrition, and movement. Through this approach, she has overcome her own symptoms and now helps others achieve lasting wellness. Helen also loves cooking and teaching people how to easily incorporate anti-inflammatory foods into their diets.

# Transforming Your Health with Nutrition and Lifestyle Medicine

By Helen Ross

This is my story.

Growing up in 1970s suburban Melbourne, Australia, my childhood diet reflected the era: a mix of home-cooked meals and heavily processed foods. My mum prepared meals from scratch most days, ensuring there were vegetables on our plates. But, like many families, we also ate plenty of white sliced bread and sugary snacks. I had a particular weakness for sweets, and to make matters even more tempting, my dad managed a nearby ice cream factory. I often visited him after school and indulged in scoops of ice cream or spent the loose change he gave me on more sugary treats.

I had battled ear infections as a young child, with course after course of antibiotics, which may have set the tone for my gut health issues later in life.

At around 16, my interest in cooking and healthy eating began to emerge, but it took years before I realised that nutrition would become my career path. As a young child, I dreamt of becoming a doctor, but life led me in a slightly different direction. Today, as a registered nutritionist, I often feel my work mirrors that of a doctor—though instead of prescribing pharmaceutical drugs, I recommend dietary changes, lifestyle adjustments, and nutritional or herbal supplements. My journey to this career, however, was shaped by my own personal health struggles.

As an adult, I struggled for years with digestive issues, including food intolerances, and irritable bowel syndrome (IBS). The symptoms ranged from bloating and abdominal pain to constipation and extreme lethargy. My twenties and thirties were marked by discomfort and frustration.

Even small amounts of certain foods—like a drop of soy sauce containing wheat—could leave me doubled over in pain. I became entirely intolerant to wheat and struggled to find relief even after adopting a strict gluten-free diet. Sugar, fruit, and alcohol also triggered symptoms, compounding my sense of helplessness.

Despite these challenges, doctors offered little guidance. My IBS diagnosis came with the disheartening message that "nothing much could be done." This lack of answers triggered a determination in me to uncover the root causes of my health problems. A conversation in 2010 about breath testing for fructose malabsorption sparked my curiosity and deepened my resolve to understand the complexities of my digestive issues.

Eventually, I decided to formalise my passion by pursuing a degree in nutrition. This choice wasn't easy; at the time, I was a full-time single mother raising my beautiful son while juggling multiple responsibilities. Along with studying part-time, running a small business, working part-time, and renovating a house, my life was hectic. My energy was often fuelled by coffee and sugar, which only exacerbated my symptoms. Stress was a huge factor, but my determination to complete my studies outweighed the challenges.

The journey to better health wasn't linear. While removing wheat from my diet initially helped, my symptoms persisted. Further exploration revealed underlying issues like small intestinal bacterial overgrowth (SIBO), intestinal permeability (leaky gut), and an overgrowth of *Candida albicans*. Addressing these imbalances required a comprehensive approach. I realised that many clients with IBS face similar challenges; their symptoms often stem from a combination of factors rather than a single cause. Achieving balance—or homeostasis—in the body requires addressing all of these aspects holistically.

Through my education and personal research, I discovered that gut health is multifaceted. It requires more than just dietary adjustments; lifestyle changes are equally critical. Over time, I learned to slow down and listen to my body. Stress reduction techniques became essential tools in managing my health. Daily meditation and yoga practices, which I've maintained for well over a decade, have been transformative for me. These rituals helped regulate my nervous system, making me more resilient when stressful situations arise. I can now approach them more calmly, avoiding the fight-or-flight response that once wreaked havoc on my gut.

These days, I'm mostly symptom-free as long as I adhere to my healthy lifestyle. My morning routine, which includes meditation and yoga, is non-negotiable. I usually aim for a minimum of 30 minutes, although an hour is preferable, if time permits. These practices set the tone for my day, grounding me and enhancing my overall well-being. I've also learned the importance of maintaining a balanced diet and incorporating regular exercise. These habits have restored my energy levels, leaving me feeling more energetic in my fifties than I ever did in my thirties.

I believe that a morning routine that allows for some time to yourself is key to living a healthy life. Obviously, this isn't always possible, especially for parents with young children; however, I believe that where there's a will, there's a way. Prioritising some self-care time at some point during the day is critical for managing your health, and not just for your gut health, but for all aspects of health. Stress is a modern-day killer, and managing our stress should be a priority.

I've learnt that the gut-brain connection is of vital significance, and I think that my stress overload, along with some less-than-ideal dietary choices, is likely what led to all of my health issues, therefore, while the nutrition support was important, it was the mindfulness practices that allowed my gut to heal over the long term.

As a nutritionist, I love inspiring others to also reclaim their health. Time and again, I've witnessed the life-changing impact of dietary and lifestyle interventions. Many of my clients arrive feeling hopeless, having been told there's little they can do about their IBS or other chronic conditions. I feel that I'm living proof that change is possible with the right tools and commitment. While the journey does require effort, the rewards are huge and life-changing.

One of the most common misconceptions I encounter is that people often fixate on a single diagnosis, like IBS, without recognising the broader picture. For example, SIBO is present in about 60% to 70% of IBS sufferers, but it's rarely the only issue. In my case, addressing SIBO alone wouldn't have resolved my symptoms without also tackling the leaky gut, the *Candida* overgrowth, and my stress. This is why I take a comprehensive approach in my practice, tailoring solutions to each client's unique combination of imbalances.

Time constraints are a frequent challenge for many clients, especially busy parents. I understand this struggle first-hand. However, I firmly believe that small, consistent steps can make a significant difference. Even dedicating just 10 to 15 minutes a day to mindfulness practices can transform overall health and well-being. It's about finding what works for your lifestyle and committing to it.

Looking back, I'm grateful for the lessons my health challenges have taught me. They've not only shaped my career but also deepened my empathy and understanding as a practitioner. Every setback has reinforced the importance of resilience, self-care, and holistic healing. Today, I'm honoured to guide others on their own healing journeys, helping them navigate the complexities of gut health and achieve lasting relief.

Ultimately, my story is one of transformation—not just physical but emotional and spiritual as well. By utilising a holistic approach, I've reclaimed my health and discovered a sense of purpose. My mission now is to empower others to do the same, proving that even in the face of chronic conditions, there is hope for a healthier, more vital future.

## Kathryn Ficarra

The C Group Studio, LLC

https://www.linkedin.com/in/kathrynficarra/
https://www.facebook.com/groups/leadershiponpurpose1
https://www.instagram.com/thecgroupstudio/
https://www.thecgroupstudio.com
https://www.youtube.com/@thecgroupstudio/podcasts

Kathryn has over two decades of experience at the VP level spanning diverse industries, including start-ups, gaming, and e-commerce. She is now a transformational architect who helps high-performers decode the DNA of extraordinary leadership with her proprietary innovative IMPACT Framework, a revolutionary approach to developing executive presence that goes beyond traditional leadership development. In addition to this Kathryn is a licensed facilitator for the Purpose Assessment, a science backed assessment too that enables leaders to tie their purpose to their work. She also hosts her podcast, Leadership On Purpose, highlighting those who are helping transform the way we lead and live.

# Your Presence Is Your Power: Unlocking Leadership Through the IMPACT Framework

By Kathryn Ficarra

What if I told you that your presence—the way you show up in a room, in a conversation, or even in your own life—has the power to leave an indelible mark? Here's the catch: presence without purpose is hollow. It might catch attention momentarily, but it doesn't inspire, connect, or create a lasting impact.

True leadership presence isn't just about being seen; it's about being felt. It's about showing up with intention, clarity, and authenticity. And at the heart of it all is purpose—the "why" behind everything you do. Purpose is the anchor that grounds your presence and makes it powerful. In this chapter, I'll introduce you to my IMPACT Framework, a step-by-step guide to cultivating a purposeful presence. Each pillar—Identity Alignment, Mindset Mastery, Purpose Assessment, Authority and Confidence, Consistent Embodiment, and Transformative Growth—builds on the one before it, creating a roadmap for unlocking your leadership potential in a way that feels authentic to who you are. It is what I teach my clients everyday, in fact it's my 10-week container condensed down to this one chapter. These are the highlights.

Before we dive into the framework, let me ask you this:

- Do you know what drives you as a leader?
- Are your actions aligned with your values and goals?
- When people experience your presence, does it reflect your true purpose? If you're unsure—or if you've never paused to think about these questions—you're not alone. Many of us have spent so much time trying to meet external expectations that we've lost touch with our internal compass. This chapter is about

reconnecting with that compass and using it to guide how you show up in every aspect of your life.

Let's begin.

## Section 1: Identity Alignment – The Foundation of Authentic Presence

### Who Are You When No One's Watching?

Leadership starts with knowing yourself—your values, your strengths, and the unique story that shapes how you show up in the world. Identity Alignment is the foundation of executive presence because when you're clear about who you are, every action, word, and decision becomes an extension of that clarity.

But here's the challenge: many of us haven't taken the time to truly explore our identity. We've been so focused on external validation—titles, achievements, or others' opinions—that we've lost sight of what drives us internally.

## Action Step: Define Your Leadership Compass

Take a moment to reflect on these questions:

1. What are the three core values that guide your decisions?
2. What is one experience in your life that shaped how you lead today?
3. If someone described your leadership in one sentence, what would they say versus would you want them to say?

Write these answers down. This is your leadership compass—a tool to guide you as you navigate challenges and opportunities.

## Section 2: Mindset Mastery – Rewriting Limiting Beliefs

### The Stories We Tell Ourselves Shape Our Reality

Even when we're clear on our identity, self-doubt or limiting beliefs can hold us back from fully embodying it. Mindset Mastery is about recognizing these mental barriers and replacing them with empowering beliefs that align with your identity and purpose.

## Action Step: Flip the Script

Identify one limiting belief that has been holding you back (e.g., "I'm not experienced enough" or "I'm not good at public speaking"). Now, reframe it into an empowering belief—beliefs are just decisions, but when you use the existing evidence in your life you can start to rebuild that piece of your identity (e.g., "I am constantly learning and growing" or "I have valuable insights to share, because I have seen this true in xyz"). Believe it for yourself. Repeat this new belief daily until it becomes second nature. This is a small part of what I teach but it's a good starting point.

## Section 3: Purpose – The Anchor That Grounds Your Presence

### Why Do You Lead?

Purpose is the driving force behind everything we do—it's what gives meaning to our actions and clarity to our decisions. Without purpose, leadership presence becomes performative—a hollow act of "looking the part" without truly embodying it. But when purpose is at the core of your presence, every word, action, and decision becomes intentional and impactful.

The Purpose Assessment (developed by The Purpose company) helps uncover what drives you at a deeper level by identifying where your beliefs, values, and goals are aligned—or misaligned—with how you show up as a leader. It also provides feedback on how others perceive your leadership presence, giving you a clearer picture of whether your purpose translates into impact.

## Action Step: Discover Your Leadership Purpose

Reflect on these questions:

1. What do I value most in my personal and professional life?
2. What impact do I want to have on others?
3. What legacy do I want to leave behind as a leader?

Write down your answers and look for common themes—they are clues to your purpose. (In my container, we take the 20-minute assessment and are given our own personal purpose statement which is directional for the remainder of this framework.)

## Section 4: Authority and Confidence – Your Authority is a direct connection to your confidence.

Authority isn't just about being the loudest in the room or having a title—it's about how you show up, how you carry yourself, and how others experience you. Confidence isn't a skill you "acquire"; *it's a byproduct of alignment, clarity, and action.* When you own your voice— your perspective, your expertise, your unique presence—you naturally command attention and respect.

We've all seen leaders who command a room without raising their voices. It's not because they dominate the conversation; it's because they radiate a quiet, steady certainty. True authority is not performative—it's deeply rooted in knowing who you are, what you stand for, and how you communicate that to the world.

*People trust leaders who trust themselves.* If you're second-guessing every word or shrinking in your own presence, others will feel that hesitation.

Authority is the ability to own your space, speak decisively, and project a presence that says, "I belong here."

One of the biggest misconceptions about authority is that it's about talking more. In reality, the most powerful leaders don't just speak with clarity—they listen with intention. Active listening signals confidence because it shows that you don't need to prove yourself with endless words. You're comfortable enough in your own authority to hold space for others.

## Action Step: Intentional Presence

In your next conversation, resist the urge to fill silence. Pause. Own your space. Speak with intention. Let your authority come from within, not from the need to prove anything.

Authority isn't just something you have—it's something you embody. And when you do, people will listen.

## Section 5: Consistent Embodiment – Aligning Actions with Values

### Leadership Is Lived Every Day

Consistency is what separates good leaders from great ones. It's not enough to show up powerfully in one meeting if your actions don't align elsewhere. Consistent Embodiment means stepping into the version of you that embodies the elements that reflect your values.

### Action Step: Create Your Leadership Alter Ego

Identify an alter ego that you authentically connect to. What are five things that your desired leadership alter ego exudes that you currently don't have? Then look at the person you are today and bridge the gap. Step into the version of you that embodies the aspects that you desire.

## Section 6: Transformative Growth – Using Your Presence to Inspire Change Your Presence Is Bigger Than You Think

When all the pillars come together—identity alignment, mindset mastery, purpose, authority and confidence, consistent embodiment—you don't just transform yourself; you transform those around you. This is Transformative Growth, where your presence becomes a catalyst for positive change within teams, organizations, and communities.

### Define Your Legacy

Ask yourself: What impact do I want my leadership to have on others? Write down three ways your presence can inspire growth in those around you—and take one action this week to make it happen.

### Closing Thoughts: Your Presence Is Your Power

Your presence isn't just something people notice when you walk into a room—it's something they feel long after you've left. By embracing the six pillars of the IMPACT Framework, you can step into any space with confidence—not just because of what you know or what you've achieved but because of who you are at your core.

Use your presence as a force for empowerment—not just for yourself but for everyone around you.

## Hayley Chambers

Animal Instincts Australia and Outback Equines
Transformative Coach, Counsellor & Facilitator

https://www.linkedin.com/in/hayleyachambers/
https://www.facebook.com/animalinstinctsaustralia
https://www.instagram.com/animalinstinctsaust/
www.animalinstinctsaustralia.com
www.outbackequines.com

Hayley Chambers is a transformative coach, counsellor, author and speaker with over 25 years of experience in personal development, coaching, and animal industries. As Managing Director of Animal Instincts Australia and Outback Equines, she empowers individuals through animal and equine-assisted therapy and facilitation, blending evidence-based strategies with the wisdom of animals. Inspired by her own journey of healing through grief, Hayley uses the transformative power of animals to help clients overcome challenges, build resilience, and embrace life's unpredictability. Her programs, held on a 103-acre farm near Toowoomba, Queensland, support diverse audiences, from children with disabilities to professionals in high-stress industries. Hayley's workshops combine equine and animal-assisted therapy, team building, and leadership coaching while rehabilitating rescue animals. Living with her son and therapy animals, Hayley's passion for fostering human-animal connections continues to inspire personal growth and authentic living.

# Embrace Your Inner Mare:
# The Power of Boundaries and Self-Care

By Hayley Chambers

In a world that often celebrates self-sacrifice and busyness, learning to listen to the wisdom of horses taught me the importance of boundaries—a lesson that has changed my life. For as long as I can remember, I've been drawn to animals, especially horses. Their ability to live in harmony with their instincts always fascinated me. But it was specifically learning to listen to one particular headstrong and opinionated mare that caused me to really understand boundaries and self-care.

In the world of horses, mares are often misunderstood. The term "beware the mare" is commonplace in the horse industry! They can be seen as temperamental or difficult, but anyone who understands them well knows that mares embody an extraordinary blend of intuition, strength, and wisdom. They demand respect, communicate boundaries with clarity, and remind us of the power of honoring our inner voice. It wasn't until I truly began to listen to the lessons of the mares in my life that I discovered how vital it was to embody those traits myself. Years ago, in the midst of my horse training career, I could be quoted as saying, "I will never own a moody mare!" I now know that this was simply a reflection of where I was at personally and professionally—while I THOUGHT that I was able to hold boundaries with significant others in my life—I was actually very fluid and usually struggled to implement anything but flexibility for other's needs and wants, usually at the detriment of my own self-care.

Over the years, I often found myself caught in a whirlwind of responsibility—work, family, and the constant pressure to be everything to everyone. My days started early, filled with endless tasks, and often ended in exhaustion. The little voice inside me, whispering that something needed to change, was drowned out by the clamor of my obligations. I convinced myself that sacrificing my well-being was part of being a dedicated business owner, loving partner, and mother. But deep down, I knew I was running on empty. My body whispered warnings through exhaustion and stress, yet I ignored them, believing I could simply push through.

Kande, an Arabian mare I acquired from clients many years ago, came into my life after I started her under saddle for them, working closely with her and developing a strong bond. When she was returned home, Kande quickly made it clear that her young rider was not the right match for her! She was the ultimate stereotypical "moody mare" I had always sworn I would never own. But despite this, we seemed to just understand each other. At the time, I had recently emerged from a messy divorce and was finally gaining some traction, no longer weighed down by the burdens of a toxic marriage. That's when Kande decided I would be her new home.

After some revelations in my life and some big life lessons, standing in the paddock with Kande, I had an awakening. She was known for her strong personality—she didn't tolerate disrespect or rushed energy. If you approached her without clarity and calm, she would turn her back and walk away, often with a look of disdain on her usually pretty face! But when you met her with authenticity and respect, she would lean into the connection with grace and trust. I've always joked that Kande is not the ideal therapy horse unless you are truly ready to hear the blunt truth about where you are at in your life which is usually quite confronting! In this interaction with her, I realized I had been ignoring my own boundaries, failing to approach my life with the same clarity and respect Kande demanded. I was saying yes when I wanted to say no, pushing through exhaustion, and silencing my inner voice. Watching Kande, it became clear: I needed to embrace my inner mare.

This wasn't easy! I had to unlearn years of people-pleasing and reframe my mindset around self-care. Instead of seeing boundaries as selfish, I began to understand them as essential acts of self-respect. Like Kande, I needed to communicate my needs clearly and unapologetically. There were moments of guilt and discomfort, of course. Setting boundaries often means challenging others' expectations. But I reminded myself of Kande—how she never apologized for walking away from what didn't serve her. Her boundaries were her strength, and they allowed her to thrive.

Something amazing started to happen. The more I honored my needs, the more grounded I became. My relationships deepened because I was showing up as my authentic self—not a reduced version of me. And, most importantly, I felt a spark of vitality returning. My work became more impactful because I was operating from a place of alignment, not depletion. My relationship with my child became more grounded, less rushed, and more loving.

One of the most transformative shifts was in how I approached self-care. Before, I saw it as a luxury, something I'd get to once everything else was done. But Kande's wisdom has taught me that self-care is non-negotiable. It's the foundation that allows us to show up fully for others. I now see boundaries not as walls that separate us but as bridges that allow us to connect more meaningfully. Boundaries aren't barriers; they're invitations for respect. When a mare sets a boundary, it's not to push others away but to create space for trust and safety.

By protecting my energy, I can show up as my best self for the people and passions that matter most. Working with Kande also deepened my understanding of how to guide others. In my business, I help women learn to embrace their instincts and set boundaries. Sharing my journey with them—how I learned to be more "mare" in my approach to life— has become a key part of my coaching. It's incredible to witness the transformation that happens when women give themselves permission to say no, to rest, and to prioritize their well-being.

Kande's lessons continue to affect my life. Each time I feel the pull to overcommit or ignore my needs, I think of her standing firm, ears back, quietly asserting herself without apology. She reminds me that boundaries are an act of self-love, not selfishness. They're a way of honoring our intuition and creating space for the things that truly matter.

Today, I live my life with a newfound sense of balance and vitality. By trusting my instincts and setting boundaries, I've not only deepened my connection with myself but also with the people and animals around me. Kande's wisdom has become my own, and it's a gift I'm passionate about sharing with others.

To every woman reading this: Your inner mare is waiting for you to listen. She will guide you to a life of clarity, balance, and vitality if you let her. Trust her voice. Honor her boundaries. Just like a mare, you can stand firm in your truth, knowing that by doing so, you're creating space for authentic connection and a life that truly glows.

## Yalonda Smith

# Letting Go and Loving my Truth

By Yalonda Smith

My truth has brought me into the knowledge that there's no need to wait because everything is now. Everything that I want, desire, and need in my lifetime is already here.

Allow me to explain. One word that I was taught to believe as a child with patience. I was supposed to wait while trusting in God for what I wished and hoped for to happen. I was supposed to wait and pray to God every day about it. When in truth what I anticipated God bringing was already here. It was already present. The truth was about me being on the right frequency that would allow be on the vibration where it appeared.

The experience of family passing away positioned me to look at this truth.

There was no one left to guide me, to get advice from, to tell me the right and wrong from their perspectives (that's why they wanted them to be mine). There was no parent left that would be upset with me because I didn't follow their direction. I was free to follow my truth.

I had to shed a lot from who I had been made to believe was my truth.

This process brought on a lot of anxiety. Although, I had to do it, and the best way for me to do it was alone. I listened to my higher self, my higher power, the true voice within me. I was directed towards the truth of God. I began to completely unattach myself of misinformation and manipulation tactics that caused me to believe a certain way. The passing of my parents caused me to truly face the mirror and see my reflection.

After my parents passing, I could have dwelled in moment of grief. But the better decision for me was to learn from everything, Everything, EVERYTHING they'd taught me; separate the good from the bad, analyze it, and create who I was going to be because of their lessons. My parents were amazing, and I'm so grateful that I was their daughter. But there were some things they did and said that hurt me. But instead of allowing it to affect my life I chose to learn it.

Nothing can bother you unless you let it bother you. Nothing can get under your skin or nag at you unless you allow it. This is your life, and you must know that you are the only one in the room (you are the only person that matters). This is your life, and you choose to be here by waking up every day in it.

This year will make six years since the passing of my father and four years since the passing of my mother. I started my blog page letting go and loving my truth about 5 months before the passing of my father, and what a journey along my truth it has been.

In the past years I've felt that I need material memories to comfort me. But this is the year of reorganization. This year is about letting go and loving who I am completely, letting go and loving my peace, letting go and loving my reason for waking up every morning, letting go and loving my purpose, letting go and loving my power, letting go and loving my truth.

## Amayra Morales

Ayurveda Digestive Health Coach

https://www.facebook.com/amayra.r.morales/
https://www.instagram.com/amayramorales/
https://amayramorales.com/

Amayra spent over a decade climbing the corporate ladder until her relentless drive led to burnout and a hospital stay. After her release, she sought answers from countless specialists, but no one could explain the root cause of her symptoms. Frustrated by medication that offered no relief, Amayra began questioning her life and left the corporate world behind. Pursuing her dream of becoming a yoga teacher, she traveled to India, where a health crisis led her to an Ayurvedic clinic. This serendipitous encounter changed her life. Ayurveda helped Amayra uncover the root cause of her symptoms and reclaim her health. Inspired by its transformative power, she studied Ayurveda and discovered her true Dharma: helping women achieve glowing skin from the inside out. Amayra believes in empowering women to view their kitchen as a pharmacy, sleep as medicine, movement as healing, and mindfulness as essential self-care.

# Let's Glow with Ayurveda

By Amayra Morales

What if your body was more than just a vessel carrying you through life?

What if it was a powerful communicator, constantly whispering—or even shouting—what it needs to thrive?

For me, those whispers came in the form of insomnia, a weakened immune system, gut dysbiosis, hair loss, hyperthyroidism, candida, amenorrhea, low energy, mood swings, and rosacea. Each symptom was my body crying out for attention, even when I didn't yet know how to listen.

This chapter is dedicated to all my siSTARS who feel lost and unsure where to begin their healing journey. I see you. I feel you. I hear you.

Healing can feel like an impossible mountain to climb when answers seem out of reach. I know this because I've been there. At the height of my career as a Marketing Executive, I hit my lowest health point. Staring up at the ceiling of the hospital room, I realised something had to change. That breaking point became the turning point.

In my search for healing, I discovered Ayurveda—an ancient system of medicine that addresses the whole person: mind, body, and soul. It taught me that healing isn't linear or one-size-fits-all but a deeply personal journey of self-discovery.

This chapter is a reminder that true healing is about reclaiming your power, rediscovering your glow, and stepping into the vibrant being you are meant to be. Seven years later, I see my health challenges not as setbacks but as gifts—initiations that helped me become who I am today.

Health is not the ultimate goal. It's the foundation that empowers you to live your Dharma, dream bigger, love harder, and show up fully in life. Consumed by symptoms, it's easy to lose sight of the bigger picture: You are here to live your best life.

Let me share the wisdom that brought me back to balance and vitality, starting with simple, actionable steps to illuminate your path to wellness.

## The Foundation of Healing: Taking Radical Responsibility

If there's one lesson I've learned, it's this: no one is coming to save you. True healing begins when you take radical responsibility for your health—not with blame or shame, but with empowerment.

For me, this shift began when I stopped blaming genetics or stress and started asking deeper questions: Why was my body reacting this way? What was it trying to tell me? That mindset shift was transformative. When you own your journey, you step into your power as the creator of your health story.

## Gut Health: The Root of Radiance

Ayurveda teaches that "all disease begins in the gut," a concept now echoed by modern science. The gut is the centre of digestion, immunity, and emotional well-being. For years, my imbalanced gut was the root cause of my health struggles.

Ayurveda identifies three primary doshas—Vata (air and space), Pitta (fire and water), and Kapha (earth and water)—which influence our unique constitution and digestion. Understanding my dosha helped me tailor my diet, lifestyle, and herbal remedies to nourish my digestive fire, or "Agni."

Here's what transformed my gut health:

- Eat mindfully: Avoid distractions, chew thoroughly, and eat until satisfied, not stuffed.
- Incorporate spices: Turmeric, ginger, cumin, and fennel support digestion and reduce inflammation.

- Drink warm water: Start your day with warm filtered water to stimulate digestion and flush toxins.

Balancing my gut was the first step to radiant, glowing skin, and overall wellness.

## Daily Routines: The Key to Balance

Ayurveda emphasises Dinacharya (daily routines) to align with nature's rhythms. These routines create stability for body and mind.

Some of my favourite rituals include:

- Morning gratitude: Begin the day with stillness and gratitude.
- Tongue scraping: Detoxify and support digestion by removing toxins and bacteria from the tongue.
- Oil pulling: Swish coconut or sesame oil in your mouth for oral health and detoxification.
- Movement: Whether it's yoga, walking, or swimming, start your day with physical activity to set the tone for the rest of the day.

## Self-Care: Your Ultimate Act of Love

Self-care isn't selfish—it's essential. Ayurveda taught me that how I treat myself reflects how I value myself. Practices like abhyanga (self oil massage), journaling, or simply resting are vital for replenishing your energy and reminding yourself of your worth.

Here's how to incorporate self-care:

- Abhyanga: A warm oil massage calms the nervous system and promotes lymphatic drainage.
- Warm shower: After abhyanga, a warm shower allows the oils to nourish your skin.
- Nourishing meals: Eat warm, easy-to-digest foods tailored to your dosha (Vata, Pitta, Kapha) to create balance and vitality.

## Reconnecting with Nature

Nature is our greatest healer. Ayurveda sees humans as microcosms of the macrocosm, deeply connected to the natural world. Walking barefoot on the earth, soaking in sunlight, or breathing fresh air helps restore balance and calm the mind.

Reconnecting with nature reminded me of my place in the universe and brought peace and grounding.

## The Power of Sleep

Sleep, or "nidra," is one of Ayurveda's three pillars of health. Prioritising sleep transformed my energy and healing. Simple habits like going to bed by 10 p.m., limiting screen time, and sipping herbal teas like chamomile, Ashwagandha, and valerian root helped me rejuvenate.

Sleep isn't a luxury—it's a necessity for vibrant health.

## Hydration: Nourish from Within

Ayurveda emphasises sipping warm water or herbal teas to support digestion and detoxification. Avoid icy drinks, which can deplete your digestive fire.

Enhance hydration with lemon or Himalayan salt, and remember: Proper hydration is a simple way to flush toxins and nourish your glow.

If you want to up your hydration, try Ayurvedic Gatorade: coconut water, a pinch of salt, a squeeze of lime, and freshly grated ginger.

## Stress Management: Cultivating Calm

Stress is a major disruptor of health. Ayurveda taught me to manage my body I also had to manage my mind. Practices like meditation, deep breathing, and yoga brought calm and clarity to my life.

Stress may always exist, but how you respond to it shapes its impact. Cultivate mindfulness to move through challenges with grace.

Healing is not a destination—it's a journey of self-discovery and empowerment. It's about peeling back the layers to rediscover the vibrant, glowing version of yourself that has always been there, waiting for you to listen.

Ayurveda reminds us that healing doesn't have to be overwhelming. It's about simple, intentional steps that honour your unique constitution, your rhythms, and your needs.

It's also about compassion—understanding that every flare-up, every setback, and every challenge is not a failure but an opportunity to learn, adjust, and grow. Your body is always on your side, working tirelessly to bring you back into balance.

This is your time. Your time to glow, thrive, and shine brighter than ever before.

## Noelle Jae Robinson

Founder of The Sound Spa

https://www.linkedin.com/in/noelle-robinson-b615152a2/
https://www.facebook.com/noellejaerobinson
https://www.instagram.com/heynoellejaerobinson/
https://thesoundspa.com/

Noelle Jae Robinson is a visionary holistic wellness practitioner and founder of The Sound Spa, a sanctuary for nervous system regulation, emotional healing, and physical restoration. With a unique ability to bridge the science of wellness and the art of inner peace, Noelle integrates sound therapy, meditation, and education to empower individuals on their own journeys to wholeness. Through her dedication to nervous system regulation, she provides transformative experiences that help clients release stress, enhance emotional resilience, and reconnect with their authentic selves. Her approach blends cutting-edge neuroscience with deep respect for ancient practices, honoring the timeless wisdom of sound waves and vibration that ha supported human healing for centuries. As a passionate advocate for self-care and personal growth, Noelle has inspired countless individuals to reclaim their calm, cultivate inner strength, and live with greater intention. She is committed to guiding others toward harmony and resilience in today's fast-paced world.

# From Breaking Point to Breakthrough: The Transformative Power of Sound

By Noelle Jae Robinson

"Are you ready?" The hospital tech asked as I sat trembling in the hospital hallway.

"No," I said, tears running down my cheeks. I had spent the last two weeks being poked and jabbed for medical tests, yet the specialists still hadn't been able to find out what was happening inside my body.

I had been in pain for almost a decade. That was nothing new. However, the sudden changes to my vision and neurological functioning were alarming. I was scared. Exhausted. Defeated. And as much as I wanted answers... I also just wanted to go home and hide from it all.

I said goodbye to my husband, tears of fear streaming down my face. My mind raced with all that could go wrong throughout the procedure. *What if this causes nerve damage? What if I become paralyzed?* The thoughts may not have been rational, but they were beyond real in my world.

As I lay on the examination table, gripping its cold edges with my trembling hands, the doctor prepared for the spinal tap. Seeing my fear, he remarked, "You know you don't *have* to do this, right?"

"Yes, I do, I need to find out what is wrong." The words came out slowly. And at that moment, I stopped fighting my fears and surrendered.

I prayed for answers.

I begged for relief.

And yet, neither would come that day. My body had been crying out for help, but no one seemed to have the answers.

Each day felt like a battle against invisible forces. I was surrounded by some of the best specialists in St. Louis, and yet, nobody could give me answers for why my body felt like it was breaking down. I felt defeated. Even as the tests came back inconclusive, a quiet voice inside me refused to give up. Relief was out there—I just had to find it.

I would spend the next four years of my life searching for answers. I ate healthy. I worked out. I tried every solution I could find in a book article, and yet, the pain continued. I saw chiropractors, acupuncturists, physical therapists, and many doctors with no relief in sight.

Sometimes, I would start to feel better. But nothing took the pain and brain fog away. I spent years on an emotional roller coaster, climbing toward moments of hope only to plummet back into pain, never knowing when the next drop would come. It was a silent and lonely journey. Rarely did I articulate the depth of the pain I carried, choosing instead to mask my struggles behind a smile. Outwardly, I appeared happy and composed, but inwardly, I was longing for relief, unsure if it would ever come.

With my mind constantly racing and the pain always in the background, I began to struggle even more in my daily life. My thoughts felt like a whirlwind, darting from one worry to the next, leaving me mentally and emotionally depleted. I struggled to be fully present for my family, often feeling distracted and irritable.

At work, tasks that once felt manageable became monumental hurdles. I felt unable to keep up with the demands of middle school teaching, which only added to my sense of failure. It felt like I was failing everywhere—in my career, at home, and in my own body. Beneath the surface, I was unraveling, a hot mess barely holding it all together, desperate for a way to quiet the chaos I felt inside.

Just when I thought the chaos would never end, I stumbled upon something at a yoga retreat that would change my life forever.

A woman came and played therapeutic instruments while we all lay on the floor. She had instruments I had never really heard of before, gong and crystal bowls. From the moment the vibrations of the crystal bowls filled the room, something within me shifted. My racing thoughts began to quiet, my tense muscles softened, and for the first time in years, I felt a profound sense of calm come over me.

From that moment, I was hooked. I sought out sound baths everywhere I could find them. Within three months, I was pain-free and off all medications. It was as though the weight I had carried for years had been lifted, and my life took on a clarity I never imagined possible.

The transformation was so profound, I became determined to understand how it all worked.

*How could something as simple as sound have taken away years of pain and mental fog?*

I became obsessed with studying the science behind sound therapy—how vibrations interact with the nervous system to unlock the body's innate capacity to heal. The more I explored, the more fascinated I became by its simplicity and profound impact. What had initially been a personal journey of healing evolved into a passionate calling. Leaving my career wasn't an easy decision, but it felt inevitable. It wasn't just a career shift; it was a profound commitment to bring the same peace and renewal I had found to others who desperately needed it.

Sound is far more than something we hear—it's something we feel on a cellular level. Research reveals that sound can shift the nervous system from a stressed (sympathetic) state to a calm and restorative (parasympathetic) state, enabling the body to heal and thrive. Yet, despite the constant sounds in our environment, we rarely pause to consider their effect on our well-being.

During a sound immersion—often called a sound bath—the mind is entrained in the sound waves, creating a meditative state that can be otherwise difficult to access in today's chaotic world. For most, traditional meditation feels like a struggle, requiring time and focus that busy lives don't allow. Sound therapy offers a deeply enjoyable alternative, effortlessly guiding the body and mind toward balance.

Through the therapeutic use of sound waves, we create the optimal environment for the nervous system to reset and the body's natural healing mechanisms to activate. The transformations I've witnessed in the past three years go far beyond my own healing journey. Clients have experienced everything from reduced anxiety and better sleep, to renewed emotional balance and physical restoration. Today, I feel immensely blessed to educate and share this powerful modality, both in our studio and with people across the globe online.

I would love to share this wisdom with you and offer my favorite tips for starting your healing journey with sound and vibration today. Please scan the QR code below to access our FREE resources. Your future self will thank you! Remember.... It's never too late to heal.

# JOIN THE MOVEMENT!
## #BAUW

## Becoming An Unstoppable Woman
## With She Rises Studios

She Rises Studios was founded by Hanna Olivas and Adriana Luna Carlos, the mother-daughter duo, in mid-2020 as they saw a need to help empower women worldwide. They are the podcast hosts of the *She Rises Studios Podcast* and Amazon best-selling authors and motivational speakers who travel the world. Hanna and Adriana are the movement creators of #BAUW - Becoming An Unstoppable Woman: The movement has been created to universally impact women of all ages, at whatever stage of life, to overcome insecurities, and adversities, and develop an unstoppable mindset. She Rises Studios educates, celebrates, and empowers women globally.

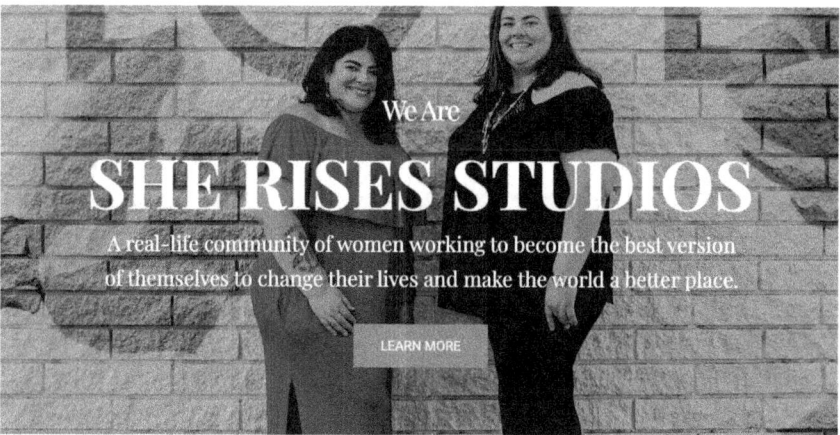

# Looking to Join Us in our Next Anthology or Publish YOUR Own?

She Rises Studios Publishing offers full-service publishing, marketing, book tour, and campaign services. For more information, contact info@sherisesstudios.com

We are always looking for women who want to share their stories and expertise and feature their businesses on our podcasts, in our books, and in our magazines.

## SEE WHAT WE DO

**OUR PODCAST**          **OUR BOOKS**          **OUR SERVICES**

Be featured in the Becoming An Unstoppable Woman magazine, published in 13 countries and sold in all major retailers. Get the visibility you need to LEVEL UP in your business!

Have your own TV show streamed across major platforms like Roku TV, Amazon Fire Stick, Apple TV and more!

Learn to leverage your expertise. Build your online presence and grow your audience with FENIX TV.
https://fenixtv.sherisesstudios.com/

Visit www.SheRisesStudios.com to see how YOU can join the #BAUW movement and help your community to achieve the UNSTOPPABLE mindset.

Have you checked out the *She Rises Studios Podcast?*

Find us on all MAJOR platforms: Spotify, IHeartRadio, Apple Podcasts, Google Podcasts, etc.

**Looking to become a sponsor or build a partnership?**

Email us at info@sherisesstudios.com

SHE RISES
STUDIOS